# New French Table

Emily & Giselle Roux

# New French Table

A fresh take on classic recipes

MITCHELL BEAZLEY

An Hachette UK Company
www.hachette.co.uk

First published in Great Britain in 2017 by Mitchell Beazley,
a division of Octopus Publishing Group Ltd, Carmelite House,
50 Victoria Embankment, London EC4Y 0DZ

www.octopusbooks.co.uk

Design and layout copyright © Octopus Publishing Group 2017
Text copyright © Emily & Giselle Roux 2017
Photography copyright © Helen Cathcart 2017

ISBN 978-1-78472-221-0

A CIP catalogue record for this book is available from the British Library.

Printed and bound in China

10 9 8 7 6 5 4 3 2 1

Commissioning Editor:
    Eleanor Maxfield
Senior Editor: Leanne Bryan
Art Director: Juliette Norsworthy
Photographer: Helen Cathcart
Food Stylist: Rosie Birkett
Props Stylist: Linda Berlin
Production Manager:
    Caroline Alberti

To Raymonde, grandmother and mother...

# Contents

Introduction

# How to Use This Book

This is the story of a mother and daughter's culinary lives and it reflects how their food has evolved over the years.

The journey starts with soups and salads. Emily was brought up on the colourful and wholesome soups that her mother would prepare all year round. The same ethos applies to Giselle's salads – never boring, always delicious. One of their favourite recipes is the tantalizing Fregola, Chorizo and Roasted Pepper Salad on page 54, which showcases the bold colours and flavours that they enjoy using and eating.

Next, we explore the southern French food that Giselle ate as a child and later cooked for her family and friends, then moving on to the imaginative, modern dishes that Emily now makes. Emily has introduced her mother to new dishes and techniques gleaned from her travels and her experiences in restaurant kitchens worldwide, but which all stem from her family's love of cooking and sharing food.

The all-important chapter on bread-making reflects their family traditions, with recipes that Giselle learned from her own mother, using her special Mother Dough starter (*see* page 228). The Rye Bread with Walnuts and

Raisins on page 232 is a staple for Giselle, who makes it to eat at breakfast or to serve with cheese.

The book ends – like every good meal – with dessert. When it comes to the sweet course, mother and daughter agree that classic dishes are best, so this chapter includes many dishes that Giselle ate as a child and that the whole family still enjoy.

This is a unique record of a family kitchen and of cooking skills passed from generation to generation. And, now, with Emily passing on her professional knowledge to her mother, the story has come full circle.

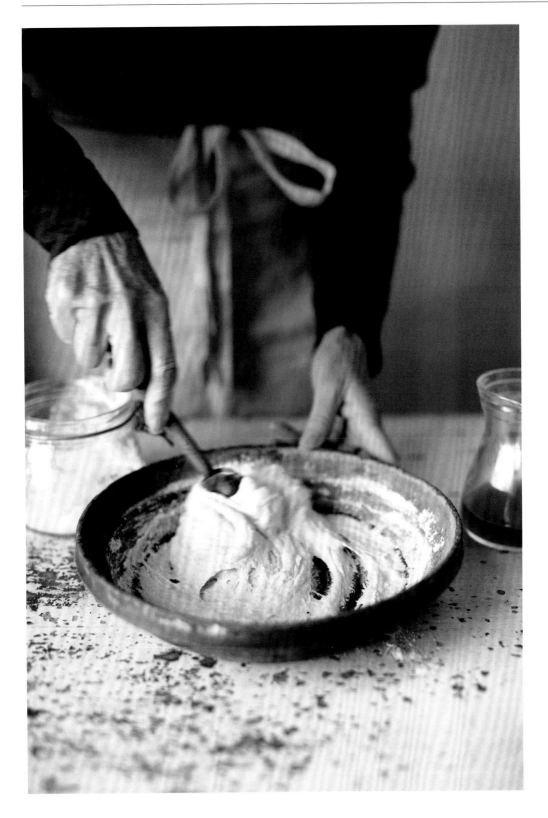

# Giselle

We are a foodie family – we love to cook and we love to eat. I grew up in a typical French household where we ate good, traditional, southern French food. I then married into the Roux family and became part of a cooking dynasty.

Food has always been, and still is, a big part of my life, but I had never thought of writing a book about it. One day when I was grumbling to my husband Michel that he had stolen yet another of my recipes for his book, his reply was: 'Well, write your own then!' I didn't take him seriously at first – I am a home cook, not a professional, so a cookbook seemed out of the question.

When our daughter Emily came back to live in London after attending catering college in Lyon and working in various prestigious restaurants we came up with a brilliant idea – a mother and daughter cookbook. We decided to combine my background of French home cooking with Emily's professional expertise and enthusiasm for the new techniques and contemporary tastes. I understand how the home cook feels and works, while Emily knows how to explain what to do.

We have both learned a lot and had so much fun coming up with the recipes for this book. We have worked through from the dishes I enjoyed as a child, to the food I cooked for Emily when she was growing up, then finally, to the meals we make together today.

# Emily

Born into the most gastronomic of families and raised in London, my passion for food started at a young age. Playing with pots and pans instead of dolls seemed to be the norm for me. My mother always took great pleasure in providing me with fresh and healthy French food.

Many people think of French food as very rich, packed with butter and cream, but that is the northern style. The food of the South, where my mother comes from, is much closer to that of the Mediterranean, with an emphasis on fish, vegetables and olive oil.

I left the UK at the age of 18 to train at the renowned Institut Paul Bocuse in Lyon. After graduating I worked my way through the difficult echelons of a kitchen brigade in several Michelin-starred restaurants all over France. Some of these professional kitchens gave me the opportunity to travel all over the world. Today I love using the latest ingredients and innovative cooking techniques to bring a new twist on classic recipes.

In this book we show how cooking in our family has come full circle - my mother was taught by her own mother and she has now passed down her knowledge to me.

# Soups

# Giselle

Sometimes all you need is a bowl of soup: it warms you, it's healthy and what's more, it's a great way of using up vegetables, even those that are slightly past their best. I've always eaten a lot of soup and, growing up, my mother would serve it at the start of every meal during autumn and winter. She always had plenty of home-grown vegetables to hand and would make many different kinds of soup from them.

I've continued the tradition and Emily was brought up eating nourishing soups. I like to stick to one or two vegetables as a rule and let their taste shine through, rather than piling in a mishmash of lots of different sorts, then build up layers of flavour with ingredients such as ginger, chestnuts and walnuts. The flavours I use are more adventurous than my mother's and Emily has always appreciated them, even when she was a small child. These days, I'm even more daring and enjoy making things like Sweetcorn Soup with Popcorn and Crispy Chicken Skin (*see* page 32). But the same waste-not-want-not values that my mother instilled in me are still at the heart of my soup making and recipes like our Radish Top Soup (*see* page 28) are testament to that.

# Green Booster Soup

*This soup is packed full of flavour and bursting with vitamins; the perfect pick-me-up for a cold winter's evening.*

**serves 4**

1 tablespoon olive oil,
  plus extra for drizzling
½ onion, finely sliced
3 garlic cloves, crushed
2 courgettes, sliced
400g (14oz) leeks, sliced
200g (7oz) cavalo nero
  or kale
200g (7oz) spinach

500ml (18fl oz) water
1 bunch of coriander,
  leaves chopped
1 bunch of parsley, leaves
  chopped
salt and freshly ground
  black pepper
crusty bread, to serve

Place the oil in a large pan or stovetop casserole dish over a medium heat. Once hot, add the onions and garlic and cook, stirring continuously, until tender. Add the chopped courgettes and leeks to the pan and cook, stirring, for approximately 5 minutes. After they have released most of their water, add the cavalo nero and spinach to the pan and stir to combine. Add the water, bring to a gentle simmer and leave to cook for 8 minutes.

Once all the ingredients are thoroughly cooked, season to taste and remove the pan from the heat. Transfer the soup to a blender along with both bunches of herbs (this may need to be done in batches), reserving a few leaves to garnish. Blend the soup until smooth, then transfer to serving bowls. Drizzle with good-quality olive oil and garnish with the reserved herbs. Serve very hot, accompanied by crusty bread.

# White Winter Soup

*This velvety white soup has a beautifully delicate flavour and makes the*
*perfect winter warmer when served with roasted chestnuts.*

**serves 4**

2 tablespoons butter
1 onion, finely chopped
1 celeriac (approx. 650g/
  1lb 7oz), peeled and cut
  into bite-sized chunks
570ml (1 pint) milk
250ml (9fl oz) water

1 sage leaf
1 thyme sprig
200g (7oz) peeled and
  cooked chestnuts
pinch of freshly grated
  or ground nutmeg
salt and freshly ground
  black pepper

Place 1 tablespoon of the butter in a large
pan over a medium heat. Once melted, add
the onion and cook, stirring continuously, for
about 2 minutes until soft and translucent.
Add the celeriac to the pan and cook, stirring
occasionally, for a few minutes, until it has
just started to take on some colour. Add the
milk and water to the pan, along with the
sage leaf and thyme sprig. Bring to a gentle
simmer and leave to cook, uncovered, for
25 minutes, until the celeriac is tender.

Meanwhile, melt the remaining butter in a
small pan over a low heat. Once melted, add
the chestnuts to the pan and stir to coat in the
butter. Cook gently for 2–3 minutes, until the
chestnuts are heated all the way through. Set
aside and keep warm.

Once the celeriac is tender, remove the
herbs from the pan and discard. Transfer
the soup to a blender (this may need to be
done in batches) and blend until completely
smooth. Season the soup to taste with salt,
pepper and a pinch of nutmeg, then transfer
to serving bowls. Serve the soup hot with the
chestnuts on top.

# Minestrone with Orzo

*This comforting soup is a great way to use up any leftover vegetables that are lurking in the fridge. Feel free to adapt the recipe to use what's in season and what you have to hand.*

**serves 4**

2 tablespoons extra-virgin olive oil, plus extra for drizzling
1 red onion, finely chopped
1 garlic clove, crushed
1 carrot, peeled and diced into 1cm (½ inch) cubes
1 celery stalk, finely sliced

4 baby courgettes, diced into 1cm (½ inch) cubes
100g (3½oz) French beans, sliced into quarters
1 thyme sprig, leaves picked
450ml (16fl oz) vegetable stock
200g (7oz) tinned chopped tomatoes

50g (1¾oz) orzo
40g (1½oz) baby watercress
1 handful of fresh parsley leaves, roughly chopped
salt and freshly ground black pepper

Heat the olive oil in a large pan over a medium heat. Once hot, add the onion, garlic, carrot, celery, baby courgettes, French beans and thyme to the pan and sauté, stirring continuously, for 5 minutes. Pour the vegetable stock and tinned tomatoes into the pan and stir to combine. Bring to the boil, then reduce the heat to a simmer and season to taste. Add the orzo to the pan and stir to combine. Leave to cook for around 10 minutes, until the orzo is cooked but still retains a little bite.

Divide the soup between 4 serving bowls and top with the watercress, a scattering of fresh parsley and a drizzle of extra-virgin olive oil. Serve hot.

# Mushroom Velouté with Roasted Spiced Walnuts

*The spiced walnuts in this healthy recipe add a delicious crunch and a hit of spice. The walnuts can be made ahead and are delicious enjoyed on their own as a moreish snack.*

**serves 2**

**For the velouté:**
2 tablespoons olive oil
500g (1lb 2oz) chestnut
  mushrooms, roughly
  chopped
1 large onion, finely
  sliced
1 garlic clove, crushed
1 tablespoon butter
300ml (½ pint) whole milk
salt and freshly ground
  black pepper

**For the roasted spiced walnuts:**
1 tablespoon egg white
75g (2¾oz) shelled walnuts
pinch of chilli powder
pinch of dried rosemary
pinch of ground cumin

Preheat the oven to 190°C (375°F), Gas Mark 5 and line a baking sheet with greaseproof paper.

To prepare the roasted walnuts, place the egg whites in a bowl and lightly whisk to break them up. Add the walnuts to the bowl, followed by the spices, then mix everything together to ensure the nuts are well coated. Spread the walnuts out on the prepared baking sheet and bake for 5–8 minutes. Once cooked, set aside until ready to use.

Meanwhile, prepare the velouté. Heat the olive oil in a large frying pan over a high heat. Add the mushrooms and cook, stirring continuously, for 3 minutes, until lightly browned and most of their water has been released. Add the onions, garlic and butter to the pan and reduce the heat to medium. Continue to cook, stirring, for a further 3 minutes, until the onions are soft and translucent. Season to taste, then add the milk to the pan and stir to combine. Just as the milk is starting to simmer, remove the pan from the heat and transfer the contents to a food processor. Blend the mixture until completely smooth.

Divide the velouté between 2 serving bowls and garnish with the roasted walnuts. Serve hot.

# Split Pea Soup with Crispy Lardons and Croutons

*This is a hearty and satisfying soup that is made even more tempting by the crunch of crispy croutons and salty bacon lardons. One bowl will keep you going all day.*

**serves 4**

**For the soup:**
2 tablespoons olive oil
3 leeks (approx. 300g/
  10½oz), roughly chopped
2 onions, finely sliced
250g (9oz) dried split
  peas, soaked overnight
  in water, then drained
  and rinsed

2 teaspoons salt
1.4 litres (2½ pints)
  water
150g (5½oz) smoked lardons

**For the croutons:**
3 slices stale white bread
  (approx. 180g/6oz), cut
  into 1.5cm (⅝ inch)
  cubes

1 thyme sprig, leaves
  picked
1 garlic clove, crushed
2 tablespoons olive oil
salt and freshly ground
  black pepper

Preheat the oven at 180°C (400°F), Gas Mark 4 and line a large baking sheet with greaseproof paper.

To make the soup, heat the olive oil in a large pan over a medium heat. Add the leeks and onions and cook, stirring continuously, for 10 minutes, until soft and translucent. Add the split peas, salt and water to the pan and bring to a boil. Once boiling, reduce the heat to a simmer and leave to cook, covered, for 45–50 minutes, stirring occasionally.

Meanwhile, prepare the croutons. Place the cubes of bread, thyme and garlic in a bowl and season with salt and pepper. Drizzle over the olive oil, then toss everything together with your hands to ensure that the croutons are well coated. Spread the croutons out in a single layer on the prepared baking sheet and

transfer to the oven for 15 minutes, turning halfway through cooking, until crispy and golden. Set aside until ready to use.

Place a nonstick frying pan over a medium heat and, once hot, add the lardons and cook, stirring continuously, for 4–5 minutes, until crispy and golden brown. Set aside until ready to use.

Once the soup has cooked, transfer to a blender (this may need to be done in batches) and blend to a consistency that you are happy with – we prefer ours to retain a little chunkiness rather than being completely smooth.

Divide the soup between 4 serving bowls and garnish with the crispy croutons and lardons. Serve piping hot.

# Radish Top Soup

*Never throw your radish tops away; they are packed with flavour and*
*can easily be turned into a delightful and very economical soup.*

**serves 2**

300g (10½oz) radish tops
2 tablespoons olive oil,
  plus extra for drizzling
2 onions, finely sliced
1 large potato (approx.
  200g/7oz), peeled and
  finely sliced
1 teaspoon dried or fresh
  thyme
1 tsp salt
1 litre (1¾ pints) chicken
  stock
freshly ground black
  pepper

To prepare the radish tops, soak them for 15 minutes in a large quantity of water, drain and soak again until no grit or dirt remains. Transfer the radish tops to a salad spinner to remove any excess water.

Heat the olive oil in a large pan over a medium heat. Once hot, add the onions and potato, followed by the thyme, salt and a grinding of pepper. Cook the vegetables, stirring continuously, for around 5 minutes, until the onions are soft and translucent. Add the chicken stock to the pan, bring to a gentle simmer and leave to cook for 5 minutes, until the potato slices are tender.

Once the potatoes are cooked through, add the radish tops to the pan and cook for 3 minutes more, stirring occasionally. Transfer the soup to a blender (this may need to be done in batches) and blend until completely smooth. Check the seasoning and adjust if necessary, then transfer to serving bowls, drizzle with olive oil and serve hot.

# Butternut Squash, Garlic and Coriander Soup

*The tangy combination of fresh ginger, garlic and coriander brings this simple and delicious recipe together.*

**serves 2**

1 butternut squash (approx. 600g/1lb 5oz), peeled and cut into bite-sized chunks
3 garlic cloves, halved
1 tablespoon grated fresh root ginger
1 thyme sprig
1 litre (1¾ pints) water or chicken stock
2 teaspoons sea salt flakes
1 pinch of chilli powder
olive oil, for drizzling
1 handful of coriander leaves, chopped, to garnish

Place the squash, garlic, ginger and thyme sprig in a large pan and pour over the water or chicken stock. Place the pan over a medium heat and bring to the boil. Add the salt and chilli powder, then reduce the heat to low and leave to cook, covered, for around 15 minutes, or until the squash is tender.

Remove the thyme sprig from the pan and discard. Transfer the soup to a blender (this may need to be done in batches) and blend until completely smooth. Check the seasoning and adjust if necessary, then transfer to serving bowls. Serve the soup hot with a drizzle of olive oil and a scattering of coriander leaves to garnish.

# Sweetcorn Soup with Popcorn and Crispy Chicken Skin

*This combination may sound unusual, but give it a try and it's sure to become a firm favourite. The slight sweetness of the corn and the crunch of the chicken skin is a match made in heaven.* Piment d'Espelette *is a variety of pepper cultivated in the French Basque region of Espelette in the foothills of the Pyrenees. The spice has received* AOC *status* (appellation d'origine contrôlée) *for its distinctive mildly spicy, smoky-sweet flavour.*

**serves 2**

skin of 1 medium chicken
  (approx. 150g/5½oz)
2 tablespoons olive oil
1 onion, roughly chopped
1 garlic clove, crushed
280g (10oz) tinned
  sweetcorn (drained
  weight)

450ml (16fl oz) chicken
  stock
2 tablespoons vegetable oil
1 handful of popcorn
  kernels
2 pinches of *piment
  d'Espelette* or chilli
  powder
1 teaspoon salt

2 tablespoons melted
  butter
50ml (2fl oz) double cream
salt and freshly ground
  black pepper

Preheat the oven to 190°C (375°F), Gas mark 5 and line a baking sheet with greaseproof paper.

Lay the chicken skin flat on a chopping board and trim off any excess fat. Cut the skin into shards and lay flat on your prepared baking sheet. Season the skin with salt and pepper, then cover with another sheet of greaseproof paper. Lay a heavy baking sheet over the second sheet of greaseproof paper (this prevents the skin from curling up during cooking) and transfer to the oven to bake for 1 hour, until browned and crispy. Once cooked, set aside to cool.

Meanwhile, heat the olive oil in a large pan over a medium heat. Once hot, add the onion and garlic and cook, stirring continuously, for around 3 minutes, until soft and translucent. Add the sweetcorn and continue to cook, stirring, for around 3 minutes, until the liquid from the corn has evaporated. Pour in the chicken stock, bring to the boil and then reduce the heat to a gentle simmer. Cook for 15 minutes, stirring occasionally.

While the soup is cooking, prepare the popcorn kernels. Heat the vegetable oil in a large, lidded pan over a medium heat. Once hot, add half of the popcorn kernels to the pan and replace the lid. Cook, shaking the pan continuously, for 30 seconds. Once the kernels have popped, remove the lid and transfer the cooked corn to a bowl to cool. Repeat the process with the remaining corn, taking the pan off the heat after 30 seconds and leaving until all of the kernels have popped. Transfer the second batch of popcorn to the bowl, add the *piment d'Espelette* or chilli powder, salt and melted butter, and toss everything to combine. Set aside.

Once the soup has cooked, stir in the cream and season to taste. Transfer the soup to a blender (this may need to be done in batches) and blend until completely smooth. Divide the soup between 2 serving bowls and serve topped with the popcorn and shards of crispy chicken skin.

# Salads

# Giselle

When I was a child we ate salad every day in
the summer to start a meal as we grew lots of
different types of salad leaves in the garden.
We used wild leaves too, and my mother would
send us out to gather wild herbs and dandelion
leaves – probably a good way of keeping us out
of mischief!

I still make the lentil salads and Niçoise
salad that my mother loved, but over the years
I've tweaked and modernized them. I have always
been a bit of a health freak and I like to use
ingredients, such as quinoa that weren't around
when I was growing up. I usually include some
protein too, such as nuts or meat or fish, so
the salads are filling – for example, my Carrot,
Chicory and Chicken Salad with an Asian Twist
(*see* page 50), and my Fregola, Chorizo and
Roasted Pepper Salad (*see* page 54). We eat our
salads as a main meal now, which suits us all.

# Fennel, Stilton and Pine Nut Salad

*This light salad is a refreshingly crisp and crunchy addition to any meal. Packed with delicate flavours, the blue cheese perfectly complements the slight hint of aniseed in the fennel.*

**serves 4**

½ bunch of flat-leaf
  parsley (approx.
  15g/½oz)
¼ bunch of coriander
2 large bulbs of fennel
½ bunch of chives
30g (1oz) pine nuts
1 teaspoon aged balsamic
  vinegar
1 tablespoon lemon juice
2 tablespoons olive oil
70g (2½oz) Stilton
salt and freshly ground
  black pepper

Pluck the best-looking leaves off the parsley and coriander bunches and place them in a large bowl of ice-cold water. Use the remaining leaves in other recipes in the book. Top and tail the fennel, retaining the fronds for garnishing, and slice it finely lengthways; using a mandolin will make your life a lot easier (but be careful of your fingers). Place all the fennel shavings in the iced water to crisp up. After a couple of minutes dry everything in a salad spinner, then place on a large plate or in a bowl. Slice the chives into small 1cm (½ inch) pieces.

Throw the pine nuts in a dry frying pan and cook over a medium–low heat, stirring frequently until golden brown. After around 3–4 minutes remove the nuts from the heat and leave to cool on kitchen paper.

Whisk the vinegar, lemon juice and olive oil with a pinch of salt and pepper in a small bowl to make a dressing, then pour over the fennel salad and mix well. Delicately crumble the Stilton on top and sprinkle with the pine nuts, chives and reserved fennel fronds.

# Roasted Beetroot Salad with Confit Shallots and Goats' Cheese Shavings

*Roasting beetroot transforms this earthy vegetable into something silky and tender, bringing out the beetroot's sweeter side. This salad is perfect for a healthy and delicious lunch.*

**serves 2**

450g (1lb) red beetroot
250ml (9fl oz) olive oil,
  plus 2 tablespoons for
  the dressing and extra
  for drizzling
1 pinch of dried oregano
2 small shallots (approx.
  70g/2½oz), peeled

30g (1oz) walnuts, lightly
  roasted
¼ bunch of chives, roughly
  chopped
1 tablespoon good-quality
  balsamic vinegar
1 small hard goats' cheese
  (35g/1¼oz)
salt and freshly ground
  black pepper

Preheat the oven to 190°C (375°F), Gas Mark 5. Scrub the beetroot thoroughly and cut off the leaves, if there are any (keep them to add to your salad). Wrap the beetroot loosely in foil with a drizzle of olive oil, a pinch of oregano and salt and pepper. If the beetroots are small enough and roughly the same size you can put several in the same foil parcel. Place on a baking tray and roast in the oven for 1½ hours (add 30 minutes for larger veggies), or until the tip of a knife easily slides through the middle of the beetroot.

Cook the shallots at the same time as the beetroot. Place them in a small ovenproof dish with enough oil to submerge them, then cover with foil and bake in the oven for 1 hour, or until they are a light golden colour and very soft.

Remove the shallots and the beetroot from the oven. Leave the shallots to cool to room temperature. Leave the beetroot until cool enough to handle, then peel off the skins with the help of a small cloth.

Cut the beetroot into bite-sized pieces and flake or separate the shallots into a salad bowl. Add the roasted walnuts, roughly chopped chives and season with the 2 tablespoons olive oil, the balsamic vinegar, salt and pepper. Finally, crumble the goats' cheese over the top of this beautiful salad.

# Niçoise Salad with Fresh Tuna and Pesto Dressing

*This typical Mediterranean salad can be disappointing with the dry canned tuna that it is usually made with, but this recipe is a tastier interpretation of a Niçoise, with fresh tuna and a pesto dressing.*

**serves 2**

140g (5oz) new potatoes
100g (3½oz) green beans, trimmed
2 eggs
a drizzle of olive oil
180g (6oz) fresh tuna
1 tablespoon black olives, pitted

½ spring onion, finely sliced
6 cherry tomatoes, halved
2 baby gem lettuces, leaves only
1 handful of mesclun salad or baby mixed salad leaves
1 handful of small basil leaves

**For the dressing:**
1 teaspoon Dijon mustard
1 teaspoon basil pesto
2 tablespoons olive oil
1 tablespoon lemon juice
salt and freshly ground black pepper

Cook the new potatoes in boiling water for 10–15 minutes until tender, then drain and leave to cool. Cut in half or into quarters depending on the size and set aside.

Cook the beans in another pan of boiling salted water for 4–5 minutes until tender with a slight crunch. Drain and refresh in a bowl of iced water and set aside.

Fill a small saucepan with water, place the eggs in the pan and bring to the boil. Once boiling reduce the heat to a gentle simmer and set your timer for 10–12 minutes depending on how you enjoy eating your eggs. Once the eggs are cooked to your liking, remove them from the heat and refresh and peel under cold running water. Once cooled, quarter both eggs and set aside.

Heat the olive oil in a nonstick frying pan over a medium–high heat. Season the tuna with salt and pepper on both sides before putting in the pan. The fish only needs 1 minute on each side (depending on the thickness of the tuna) to stay raw and moist in the middle. Once cooked, remove from the heat and leave to cool. Slice the fish once it has cooled completely.

Delicately arrange your salad with all the prepared ingredients.

For the dressing, whisk the mustard and basil pesto together in a small bowl, then whisk in the olive oil, lemon juice and a pinch of salt and pepper. Pour the dressing over the salad.

# Quinoa Salad with Roasted Squash, Rocket and Ginger

*Served cold or warm this mouth-watering salad will convert anyone to quinoa!*

**serves 2**

½ butternut squash,
  (we like the 'coquina'
  variety) peeled,
  deseeded and cut into
  bite-sized chunks
3 tablespoons olive oil,
  plus extra for drizzling
1 sprig of thyme

1cm (½ inch) piece of
  fresh root ginger,
  peeled
90g (3¼oz) quinoa
½ shallot, finely chopped
60g (2¼oz) rocket (about
  a handful)
juice of ½ lemon
1 teaspoon Dijon mustard
15g (½oz) pumpkin seeds

10g (¼oz) sunflower seeds
salt and freshly ground
  black pepper

Preheat the oven to 190°C (375°F), Gas Mark 5.

Place the squash chunks on a baking tray with a drizzle of olive oil, salt, pepper and the thyme. Roast in the oven for 30 minutes, or until lightly coloured. As soon as you remove the baking tray from the oven, grate the fresh ginger over the top and mix together. Leave to cool.

Place the quinoa in a saucepan with double its quantity in water and simmer for 15 minutes, or until the grains swell to 3–4 times their original size. With a couple of minutes of cooking time to spare, add the chopped shallot. This will tenderize the shallot and avoid the sharpness of a raw onion. Drain the remaining water (if any) and rinse under cold water, then place in a salad bowl with the rocket and squash.

To make the dressing, whisk the lemon juice and mustard together in a bowl. While whisking, gradually incorporate the olive oil until emulsified. Season to taste with salt and pepper, then mix the dressing through the quinoa and rocket.

Dress the salad elegantly as you like and don't forget to sprinkle the seeds on top.

# Carrot, Chicory and Chicken Salad with an Asian Twist

*This salad is definitely a 'mum's special' as it is full of flavour and gives you a burst of energy for the rest of the day.*

**serves 4**

250g (9oz) boneless, skinless mini chicken breast fillets
230g (8oz) carrots, grated
1 chicory, shredded, plus a few red chicory leaves to garnish

**For the marinade:**
½ garlic clove, grated
8g (just under ¼oz) freshly grated ginger
finely grated zest of ½ lemon
5g (⅛oz) chopped coriander
1 tablespoon soy sauce
1 tablespoon sesame oil

**For the dressing:**
juice of ½ lemon
1 teaspoon Dijon mustard
2 tablespoons soy sauce
freshly ground black pepper

First, prepare the marinade as the chicken must absorb all those beautiful flavours for at least 2 hours. Slice the mini chicken breasts in half before putting them into a shallow dish. Add the grated garlic, ginger, lemon zest and coriander. Finally, combine all the ingredients together with the soy sauce and sesame oil, then cover with clingfilm and leave to marinate in the fridge.

After a couple of hours, pan-sear the chicken in a frying pan over a medium heat. You don't need to add any oil as there is enough in the marinade. Cook the fillets on each side for about 3 minutes, or until they are a lovely brown caramelized colour. Remove and leave to cool to room temperature.

Meanwhile, make the salad dressing by whisking together the lemon juice, mustard, soy sauce and black pepper in a small bowl.

In a large salad bowl, mix the grated carrots and shredded chicory together. Pour the dressing all over the raw vegetables and mix together thoroughly. Finally, slice the mini chicken fillets into bite-sized pieces, about 5mm (¼ inch) wide and spread elegantly on top of the salad. Garnish with a few red chicory leaves.

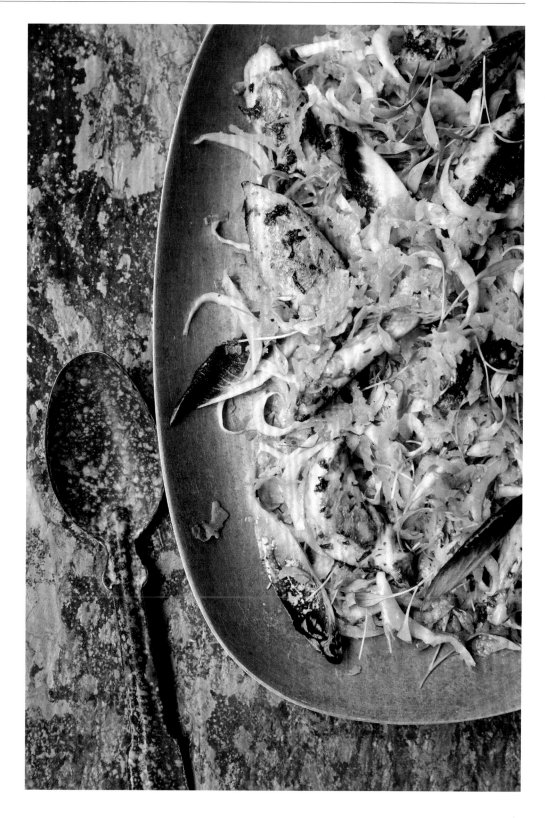

# Grilled Baby Gem and Gizzard Salad with Pickled Radishes

*Giselle: This is one of my mother's favourites because it uses her exceptional radish pickles, although she's still not sure about the warm grilled salad! You can buy duck gizzards online or, if you can't find them, then use confit duck instead.*

**serves 4**

170g (6oz) sugar snap peas
4 baby gem lettuce,
  quartered
olive oil, for brushing
425g (15oz) drained canned
  duck gizzard
1 handful of tarragon,
  leaves only
1 handful of microherbs,
  to garnish (optional)

**For the pickled radishes:**
1 bunch of radishes,
  trimmed
1 pinch of mustard seeds
1 pinch of *piment
  d'Espelette* or chilli
  powder
2 black peppercorns,
  crushed
200ml (7fl oz) water
200ml (7fl oz) white wine
  vinegar

2 teaspoons fine salt
3 tablespoons honey

**For the dressing:**
3 tablespoons cider
  vinegar
2 teaspoons Dijon mustard
1 tablespoon runny honey
170ml (6fl oz) olive oil
1 tablespoon poppy seeds
salt and freshly ground
  black pepper

To make the pickled radishes you can either slice the radishes finely with a mandolin or a sharp knife or simply quarter them, which gives them an extra crunch. Place them in a 500ml (18fl oz) jar with the mustard seeds, *piment d'Espelette* and crushed peppercorns. Bring the measured water, vinegar, salt and honey to the boil in a saucepan. As soon as it has come to a rolling boil pour the mixture directly into the jar over the radishes. Leave to cool at room temperature before use.

Blanch the sugar snap peas in a pan of boiling salted water for 2–3 minutes until tender. Drain them and then refresh them immediately in a bowl of iced water.

Brush the quartered lettuce with a little olive oil. Place a griddle pan over a high heat and char the lettuce for less than a minute. Don't cook the lettuce; just lightly smoke it.

To make the dressing, place the vinegar, mustard and honey in a small bowl. Season with a pinch of salt and pepper and whisk in the oil in a steady stream until it is combined. Finally, stir in the poppy seeds.

Arrange the sugar snap peas, lettuce and pickled radishes on plates. Slice the gizzards and scatter them over the top together with the tarragon leaves. Pour over the dressing, garnish with microherbs, if liked, and serve.

# Fregola, Chorizo and Roasted Pepper Salad

*Fregola (see photograph, pages 56–57) is a small Sardinian pasta that's rolled and toasted (resembling couscous). You can use it to make risottos, but it works perfectly in salads.*

**serves 4**

265g (9¼oz) fregola sarda
30g (1oz) sundried
  tomatoes, chopped
¼ bunch of chives, finely
  chopped
¼ bunch of parsley, finely
  chopped
1 spring onion, finely
  sliced

60g (2¼oz) chorizo,
  sliced into julienne
  (thin strips the size of
  a matchstick)
1 handful of microherbs,
  to garnish (optional)

**For the roasted peppers:**
2 red peppers, cut in half
  lengthways, stalks
  removed and deseeded
a drizzle of olive oil

salt and freshly ground
  black pepper

**For the salad dressing:**
2 whole sundried tomatoes
2 tablespoons lemon juice
1 teaspoon grated lemon
  zest
2 teaspoons wholegrain
  mustard
4 tablespoons olive oil

Preheat the oven to 200°C (400°F), Gas Mark 6 and line a baking tray with greaseproof paper.

To make the roasted peppers, place the peppers, cut-side down, on the prepared baking tray and season with salt, pepper and a drizzle of olive oil. Roast in the oven for 25 minutes until the skins are wrinkled and lightly charred. Remove from the oven, leave until cool enough to handle, then peel off the skin and slice into long strips. Set aside.

Bring a medium saucepan of salted water to the boil, add the fregola and boil for approximately 10–15 minutes until cooked through and tender. Strain and refresh under cold water. Leave to dry and cool, then place in a large salad bowl. Mix in the chopped sundried tomatoes, herbs and spring onion.

For the dressing, whisk together all the ingredients in a small mixing bowl to create a light dressing. Pour the dressing over the fregola and mix everything together. At the last minute gently fold in the roast peppers and sliced chorizo, season to taste, and garnish with microherbs, if liked.

# Lentil, Confit Tomato and Fresh Herb Salad with a Mustard Dressing

*Confit tomatoes are a great asset to any dish. You can prepare them well in advance (preferably during the tomato season) and store them in sterilized jars in olive oil in a cool place for up to a year.*

**serves 4**

200g (7oz) green lentils
1 litre (1¾ pints) water
10g (¼oz) coriander
  leaves
10g (¼oz) parsley leaves,
  roughly chopped
5g (⅛oz) mint leaves,
  chopped

15g (½oz) roasted
  hazelnuts
1 spring onion, finely
  chopped

**For the confit tomatoes:**
12 plum tomatoes (approx.
  240g/8½oz)
1 tablespoon olive oil
1 garlic clove, crushed

1 thyme sprig
1 pinch of caster sugar
salt and freshly ground
  black pepper

**For the mustard dressing:**
1 teaspoon Dijon mustard
1 tablespoon olive oil

Preheat the oven to 140°C (120°F), Gas Mark 1 and line a baking tray with greaseproof paper.

Rinse the lentils in cold water before placing them in a large saucepan with the measured water and a pinch of salt. Bring to the boil, cover the saucepan with a lid and reduce the heat to a gentle simmer for about 15–20 minutes. The lentils will double or triple in size once cooked.

For the confit tomatoes, quarter the tomatoes and remove the seeds with a small knife. (Do not discard the pulp and seeds as they will be used to make the salad dressing). Put the tomatoes in a small bowl and add the olive oil, garlic, thyme, sugar and salt and pepper. Make sure all the ingredients are properly mixed together, then spread them out on the prepared baking tray. Cook in the oven for 30–40 minutes, or until the tomatoes are slightly shrivelled and reduced in size.

Remove from the oven. Be careful as the skins will become crispy and dry.

Pluck off the tastiest looking leaves from the herbs, then roughly chop the parsley and mint leaves that are a little too big for eating whole.

As my grandmother always says, it is extremely important to use each ingredient in its integrity. Wastage does not exist in her household. Place the reserved tomato pulp and seeds in a blender together with the mustard, olive oil and a pinch of salt and blend until combined. Alternatively, simply whisk the ingredients in a jam jar. This is a tasty, easy and beautiful textured salad dressing.

Once all the components are cooled down and ready to use, gently mix the lentils and fresh herbs with the salad dressing. Finally, sprinkle the roasted hazelnuts, spring onion and the confit tomatoes on top.

# Provincial Family Food

# Emily

The recipes in this chapter are the sort of food
that mum and I enjoy cooking together. As a
family, we love southern French food - lots
of vegetables, bread and pasta, some chicken
and fish and not much red meat. People don't
always realize food in the south of France is
Mediterranean in style, using olive oil; instead
of the rich butter and cream popular in the
north of the country.

We still make the recipes I enjoyed as a child
but now I might adapt and update them. For
instance, *Lapin à la Moutarde* (*see* page 88) is a
classic that mum ate as a child and used to cook
for me in my childhood. Hers is a traditional,
rustic recipe and very good. My take on it
(*see* page 82) is slightly more refined, but
still retains all of the elements that make the
original so special. Other treasured dishes are
Tomato Tart (*see* page 75), *Tian de Legumes*
(*see* page 66), and of course *Escargots à la
Bourguignonne* (*see* page 78).

# *Tian de Legumes*

*This beautiful dish of layered roasted vegetables is a real showstopper, especially when placed in the centre of a table so that everyone can serve themselves. Equally delicious as a main course or to sit beside a joint of meat, this will have even the most committed carnivores coming back for more.*

**serves 4–6**

4 large tomatoes, cut into
  5mm (¼ inch) slices
2 red onions, cut into 5mm
  (¼ inch) slices
1 green courgette, cut
  into 5mm (¼ inch) slices
1 yellow courgette, cut
  into 5mm (¼ inch) slices

2 aubergines, cut into
  5mm (¼ inch) slices
2 teaspoons sea salt
2 garlic cloves, roughly
  chopped
1 pinch of *piment
  d'Espelette* or chilli
  powder
1 thyme sprig, leaves
  picked

5 tablespoons olive oil
40g (1½oz) Parmesan,
  grated (optional)
salt and freshly ground
  black pepper

Preheat the oven to 200°C (400°F), Gas Mark 6.

Place all of the sliced vegetables in a colander and scatter over the sea salt. Set aside for at least 20 minutes to render any excess water. Brush off the excess salt with kitchen paper and set aside.

Bring a large pan of water to the boil over a medium heat. Add the sliced vegetables and blanch for 40 seconds, then drain and lay on kitchen paper to dry. Once dry, place all of the vegetables in a large bowl with the garlic, *piment d'Espelette* or chilli powder, thyme and olive oil. Season generously, then use your hands to toss the vegetables and ensure they are all well coated in the oil and spices.

Arrange the vegetables in tight vertical rows in a large baking dish, working from the outside of the dish into the centre and alternating them to create an attractive pattern. Transfer to the oven to bake for 40 minutes, until cooked through and crispy on top. If using, scatter over the Parmesan halfway through the cooking time. Serve hot.

# *Socca*

*These chickpea flatbreads are simple to make and are an easy alternative to homemade leavened breads. They make a tasty snack served with Tapenade (see page 96), sundried tomato spread or pesto and are a great accompaniment to soups or stews.*

**serves 4**

250g (9oz) chickpea
  (gram) flour
300ml (½ pint) water
5 tablespoons olive oil,
  plus extra for greasing
½ teaspoon chopped
  rosemary
salt and freshly ground
  black pepper

Sift the flour into a large bowl and make a well in the centre. Gradually pour the water into the well, whisking the flour into the water continuously. Once the water is fully incorporated, add the olive oil and rosemary and season to taste. Whisk again to combine, then cover the bowl with clingfilm and set aside to rest at room temperature for 1 hour.

Once the mixture has rested, give it a final whisk to ensure the flour is fully incorporated and that the mixture contains no lumps.

Lightly grease a large frying pan with oil and place it over a medium heat. Once the pan is hot, pour a ladleful of the batter into the pan, swirling to cover the entire base. Cook for 2 minutes, until bubbles start to appear in the batter, then carefully flip the flatbread over in the pan and cook for another minute on the reverse side. Keep warm in a low oven while you make the remaining flatbreads (the mixture makes 5 or 6, depending on size).

Slice the breads into wedges and serve hot with tapenade, sundried tomato spread or pesto, or to accompany soups or stews.

# Whole Roasted Pigeon with Peaches, Turnips and Sage

*This roast is bursting with bold flavour combinations and the subtle sweetness of ripe peaches combined with the delicate earthiness of turnip elevates it to another level.*

**serves 2**

2 tablespoons olive oil
2 whole wood pigeons
2 thyme sprigs
2 garlic cloves, crushed
3 tablespoons butter
2 juicy peaches or
  nectarines, peeled and
  cut into bite-sized
  pieces

2 baby gem lettuce, halved
250ml (9fl oz) chicken
  stock
4 medium-sized turnips,
  halved
4 sage leaves, finely
  chopped
salt and freshly ground
  black pepper

Preheat the oven to 180°C (350°F), Gas Mark 4.

Heat a tablespoon of the olive oil in a large frying pan over a medium–high heat. Place the pigeons breast-side down into the pan, and turn every 3 minutes to evenly sear and achieve a golden colour all over. Transfer the birds, breast-side up, to a roasting pan. Season the pigeons with salt and pepper and fill their cavities with a sprig of thyme, crushed garlic clove and 1 tablespoon of butter. Transfer to the oven and roast for 10–12 minutes, depending on the size of your birds. Once cooked, remove from the oven and set aside to rest for at least 5 minutes before carving.

Meanwhile, heat the remaining olive oil in a large frying pan and, once hot, add the peaches or nectarines and lettuce halves. Cook for 2–3 minutes, turning occasionally, until the fruit is lightly caramelized and the lettuce is lightly charred. Remove from the heat and set aside.

Place the stock and remaining tablespoon of butter in a medium saucepan over a high heat. Bring just to the boil, then reduce the heat to a simmer and add the turnips to the pan. Cook, covered, for 6–8 minutes, then remove the lid and cook for a further 4 minutes, until the liquid is reduced and the turnips are beautifully glazed.

Place each pigeon on a serving plate and arrange the peaches, lettuce and turnips around the plates. Spoon over the reduced sauce and scatter the sage leaves over the vegetables. Serve hot.

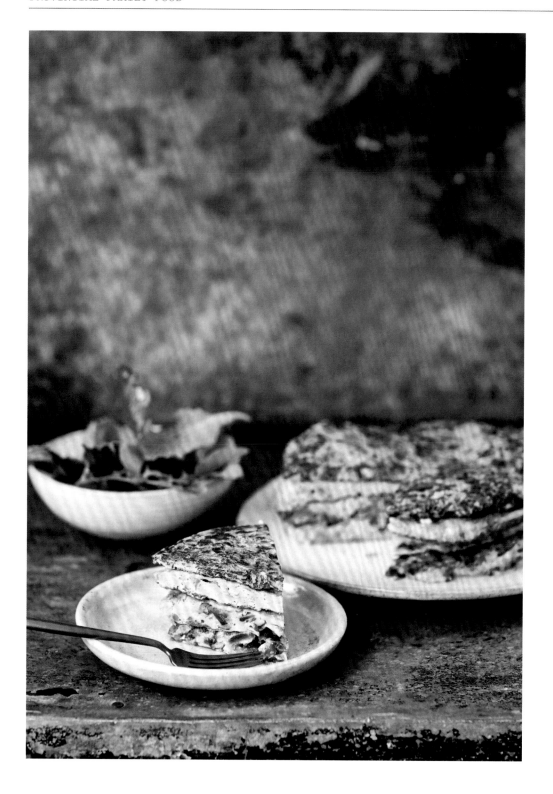

# Le Crespeou

*This is a layered omelette cake with beautiful colours and distinct flavours. Don't shy away from the work involved as it's well worth it. This is delicious eaten warm or cold with a crisp, green salad.*

**serves 6**

**For the green omelette:**
2 tablespoons olive oil
1 garlic clove, finely
  chopped
280g (10oz) baby spinach
4 eggs, beaten
salt and freshly ground
  black pepper

**For the yellow omelette:**
1 yellow pepper, halved,
  deseeded and coarsely
  grated
2 tablespoons olive oil
1 pinch of curry powder
4 eggs, beaten

**For the mushroom omelette:**
2 tablespoons olive oil
200g (7oz) white
  mushrooms, finely sliced
1 teaspoon dried thyme
4 eggs, beaten
30g (1oz) fresh grated
  Parmesan

**For the red omelette:**
3 ripe tomatoes
2 tablespoons olive oil
1 red onion, diced into
  1cm (½ inch) cubes
1 pinch of cayenne pepper
4 eggs, beaten

Start by preparing the filling for each omelette.

For the **green omelette**, heat half the olive oil in a frying pan over a medium heat and, once hot, add the garlic. Cook, stirring continuously, for 1 minute, until just starting to colour, then add the spinach and season with salt and pepper. Cook, stirring, for 3 minutes, until the spinach is completely wilted. Transfer the spinach to a bowl and set aside until cool enough to handle. Once cooled, squeeze the spinach in your hands to remove any excess water, then roughly chop. Set aside.

For the **yellow omelette**, lay the grated pepper in a piece of kitchen paper and squeeze tightly to remove any liquid. Heat half the olive oil in a frying pan over a medium heat and, once hot, add the pepper. Cook, stirring continuously, for 3 minutes, until tender, then add the curry powder and season to taste. Transfer to a plate lined with kitchen paper and set aside until ready to serve.

Continues over the page...

## *Le Crespeou* **continued**

For the **mushroom omelette**, heat half the oil in a frying pan and, once hot, add the mushrooms and thyme. Cook, stirring continuously, for 4–5 minutes, until the mushrooms are soft and have rendered all of their water. Season to taste and set aside until ready to use.

For the **red omelette**, lightly score crosses into the base of the tomatoes then place in a pan of boiling water for 20–30 seconds, until the tomato skins start to split. Drain the tomatoes, then transfer to a bowl of iced water until cool enough to handle. Peel the tomatoes and discard the skin, then slice into quarters and deseed with a spoon. Chop the tomato quarters into a 1cm (½ inch) dice and set aside.

Heat half the oil in a frying pan over a medium heat and, once hot, add the onion. Cook, stirring continuously, for 2 minutes, until just tender. Add the tomatoes and cayenne pepper to the pan and season to taste. Cook for 1 minute more, then transfer to a plate lined with kitchen paper and set aside until ready to use.

To cook the omelettes, place the beaten eggs in 4 separate bowls and add one set of your prepared fillings and some salt and pepper to each. Working with one omelette at a time, heat 1 tablespoon of oil in a frying pan and, once hot, pour in your omelette mix, swirling to ensure it coats the base of the pan. Cook for 3 minutes, until the edges are firm, then use a spatula to carefully flip the omelette and cook for a further 2 minutes on the reverse. For the mushroom omelette, add the grated Parmesan to the pan just before the omelette is flipped. Once golden on both sides, transfer the omelettes to a plate stacking them one on top of the other.

Serve the *crespeou* warm or cold with a crisp green salad.

# Tomato Tart

*This summery tomato tart is deliciously fresh and makes a wonderfully light alternative to pizza. Perfect for sharing with family and friends over a glass of wine.*

**makes a 24 × 18cm (9½ × 7 inch) tart**

350g (12oz) cherry tomatoes, halved or quartered, depending on size

3 tablespoons olive oil, plus extra for greasing and drizzling

6 small shallots, peeled and cut into 5mm (¼ inch) slices

250g (9oz) puff pastry

100g (3½oz) crème fraîche

2 tablespoons wholegrain mustard

5 basil leaves

15g (½oz) pine nuts, toasted

30g (1oz) Parmesan shavings

salt and freshly ground black pepper

Preheat the oven to 180°C (350°F), Gas Mark 4.

Place the tomatoes in a colander and generously sprinkle with salt. Set aside for 30 minutes to render any excess water. This will prevent your finished tart from being soggy.

Generously grease a baking sheet with olive oil and lay the sliced shallots over it in a single layer. Transfer to the oven and bake for 15 minutes, until just golden. Set aside until ready to use.

Lightly grease a 24 × 18cm (9½ × 7 inch) lipped baking tray with olive oil and line with greaseproof paper. On a lightly floured surface, roll out the puff pastry to the size of your tray, then transfer to the tray and lightly prick the base and sides. Cook in the oven for 10 minutes, until just golden. Remove from the oven and lower the temperature to 150°C (300°F), Gas Mark 2.

In a small bowl, whisk the crème fraîche and mustard together until just combined. Leaving a 2.5cm (1 inch) gap all around the edge of the pastry, spread the crème fraîche and mustard mix over the base of the tart. Scatter the basil leaves over the crème fraîche, then top with the tomatoes and shallots, arranging them in an attractive pattern. Return the tart to the oven to bake for another 20 minutes, until the pastry is golden and well risen and the tomatoes are soft.

Leave the tart to cool slightly, then garnish with pine nuts, Parmesan shavings and a drizzle of olive oil before serving.

# Stuffed Courgettes

*Courgettes are often overlooked, but when treated well they are packed with flavour. Here they are stuffed with a mixture of lean minced pork and sausage meat and served with a deliciously rich veal jus.*

**serves 4**

2 large courgettes
1 teaspoon olive oil
1 carrot, peeled and
  finely diced
1 onion, finely chopped
1 leek, finely chopped
1 garlic clove, crushed

150g (5½oz) sausage meat
150g (5½oz) minced pork
  loin
50g (1¾oz) Parmesan,
  grated
1 egg yolk
50g (1¾oz) mint leaves,
  roughly chopped
200ml (7fl oz) white wine

400ml (14fl oz) veal stock
salt and freshly ground
  black pepper

Preheat the oven to 180°C (350°F), Gas Mark 4.

Trim the courgettes and slice off the top third of their length. Finely dice the removed portions of courgette and set aside for later. Using a small spoon, scoop out the centre of the remaining courgettes to create hollow tubes, but leaving the base intact. Place the scooped innards of the courgette in a bowl with the diced courgette and set aside to use later.

Heat the oil in a large pan over a medium heat. Once hot, add the carrot, onion, leek, garlic and reserved courgettes and stir-fry for 3 minutes, until tender. Set aside until cool enough to handle.

Bring a pan of salted water to the boil over a medium heat and add the courgette tubes. Cook for 1 minute, then drain and immediately submerge in iced water to stop the cooking process. Set aside until ready to use.

Place the sausage meat and minced pork loin in a large bowl with the stir-fried vegetables, egg yolk and mint and season generously. Using your hands, mix all of the ingredients together until the vegetables are well dispersed through the meat. Using your hands or a small spoon, stuff this filling into the courgette tubes, ensuring that the filling reaches right to the bottom. Lay the courgettes in a flameproof roasting pan and transfer to the oven for 30 minutes to bake.

Once baked, remove the courgettes from the pan and place on serving plates. Place the roasting pan over a low heat and add the white wine. Using a wooden spoon, deglaze the pan, scraping away any brown juices that have caramelized at its base. Continue to cook until the wine has almost evaporated, then add the veal stock and cook for 5–10 minutes, until slightly thickened.

Serve the courgettes hot with the veal sauce.

# Escargots à la Bourguignonne

*This classic French recipe is utterly delicious, though perhaps not for those who are watching their diet. Smothered in rich butter and punchy garlic, this will delight even the most cautious of diners.*

**serves 4**

24 large canned snails
24 large snail shells
  (optional)
fresh bread, to serve
  (optional)

**For the garlic and parsley butter:**
½ shallot, roughly chopped
3 garlic cloves, roughly
  chopped
1 bunch of parsley, leaves
  roughly chopped

1 tablespoon cognac
100g (3½oz) softened
  butter
salt and freshly ground
  black pepper

Preheat the oven to 200°C (400°F), Gas Mark 6.

To make the butter, place the shallot, garlic, parsley and cognac in a blender and pulse until well combined. Add the butter to the blender and pulse again until well incorporated and bright green in colour. Season with salt and pepper and set aside.

If using snail shells, stuff the snails into the shells and lay on a baking sheet. If not, divide the snails between 4 small individual ramekins on a baking sheet. Divide the butter between the snails, either spooning it into the shells or over the snails in the ramekins, ensuring that each snail is generously covered.

Transfer to the oven for 8 minutes, until the butter has melted and looks as if it has separated. Remove from the oven and switch the grill to high. Place the snails under the hot grill and cook for a further 5 minutes, until the butter is bubbling and no longer looks separated.

Divide the snails between serving plates and serve with fresh bread alongside for dipping into the butter, if liked.

# Caillettes d'Ardeche

*These meatballs are fun and easy to prepare and make a wholesome winter dish.*
*You can source the different pieces of pork from your butcher.*

**serves 4–5**

650g (1lb 7oz) green Swiss
  chard leaves
75g (2¾oz) pork back fat
200g (7oz) pork neck
300g (10½oz) pork shoulder
75g (2¾oz) pork liver
4 garlic cloves, peeled

1 bunch of parsley, chopped
½ bunch of basil
1 thyme sprig
20g (¾oz) fine salt
8g (¼oz) ground white
  pepper
200g (7oz) pork caul fat
1 dash of white wine

Preheat the oven to 150°C (300°F), Gas Mark 2.

Blanch the chard in a pan of boiling salted water for 3 minutes, or until cooked. Drain and refresh in a bowl of iced water to keep those beautiful deep green colours.

Pass all the pork meat, including the back fat and liver, through a mincer together with the garlic and Swiss chard. Finely chop the fresh herbs and mix together with the minced meat. Season with the salt and pepper. With damp hands, divide the mixture equally into 4 or 5 balls depending on size. Rinse the pork caul fat under cold running water before laying out flat on a kitchen towel or kitchen paper. Tightly wrap each individual *caillette* with a single layer of the pork caul fat.

Place all the *caillettes* in a large ovenproof cast-iron frying pan or baking dish, drizzle the white wine over the top and bake in the oven for 30 minutes. Increase the oven temperature to 200°C (400°F), Gas Mark 6 for the last 15 minutes until lightly coloured and crispy on top. Serve immediately.

# Grilled Sardines with a Parsley Crumb

*These grilled sardines are a perfect starter to any meal. They are also delicious cooked on the barbecue.*

**serves 4 as a starter**

200g (7oz) dried
  breadcrumbs
grated zest of 1 lemon
1 bunch of flat-leaf
  parsley, finely chopped
1 garlic clove, finely
  chopped

2 tablespoons olive oil,
  plus extra for drizzling
8 fresh whole sardines,
  scaled, gutted and
  butterflied
salt and freshly ground
  pepper

**To serve:**
toasted sourdough
fresh tomatoes

Stir the breadcrumbs, lemon zest, parsley and garlic together in a large bowl. Season to taste with salt and pepper.

Preheat the grill to a medium–high heat. Brush a baking tray with a little olive oil and place the sardines, flesh-side down, onto the tray. Evenly distribute the breadcrumb mix all over the fish and place under the grill for 5–10 minutes, depending on the size of the fish, until the breadcrumbs are nice and crisp and the flesh of the sardines are just cooked through.

These are best served with toasted sourdough and fresh tomatoes.

# Rabbit with Mustard Relish

*This is a modern take on the classic* Lapin à la Moutarde
(*see page 88) that retains many of the flavours of the original dish
but makes for a much lighter meal.*

**serves 4**

12 baby new potatoes
2 rabbit loins, each cut
  in half
2 rabbit racks, each cut
  in half
2 tablespoons olive oil
20g (¾oz) butter
125ml (4fl oz) chicken
  stock

50ml (2fl oz) dry white wine
100g (3½oz) green baby
  leaf salad
100g (3½oz) purple baby
  leaf salad
salt and freshly ground
  black pepper
1 tablespoon mustard
  seeds, toasted,
  to serve

**For the mustard relish:**
200g (7oz) mustard leaves
  or wild rocket leaves
1 anchovy in oil
1 pickled onion in
  white wine vinegar
  (*see* page 200)
1 teaspoon Dijon mustard
  juice of ½ lime
100ml (3½fl oz) olive oil

Place the potatoes in a pan of salted
water, bring to the boil and cook for about
8 minutes until tender. Drain and set aside
to cool to room temperature.

To make the mustard relish, place all the
ingredients in a blender and blend until
smooth. Transfer to the fridge until ready
to use.

Season both the loins and racks of rabbit
with salt and pepper. Place 1 tablespoon of
the olive oil in large frying or sauté pan over
a medium heat. Once the oil is hot, add the
rabbit to the pan and sear until it is nice and
golden all over. Add the butter to the pan
and baste the meat until it is caramelized
and cooked through, around 12–14 minutes,
depending on the size of your rabbit pieces.
Transfer the rabbit to a board to rest, covered
with aluminium foil. Deglaze the pan with the
chicken stock and white wine and reduce for
5–10 minutes, until you obtain a light jus.

Place the salad leaves in a bowl with the
cooled potatoes and dress with the remaining
olive oil and a tablespoon of the jus. Serve
the rabbit drizzled with the remaining jus,
the mustard relish and salad alongside and
garnished with the toasted mustard seeds.

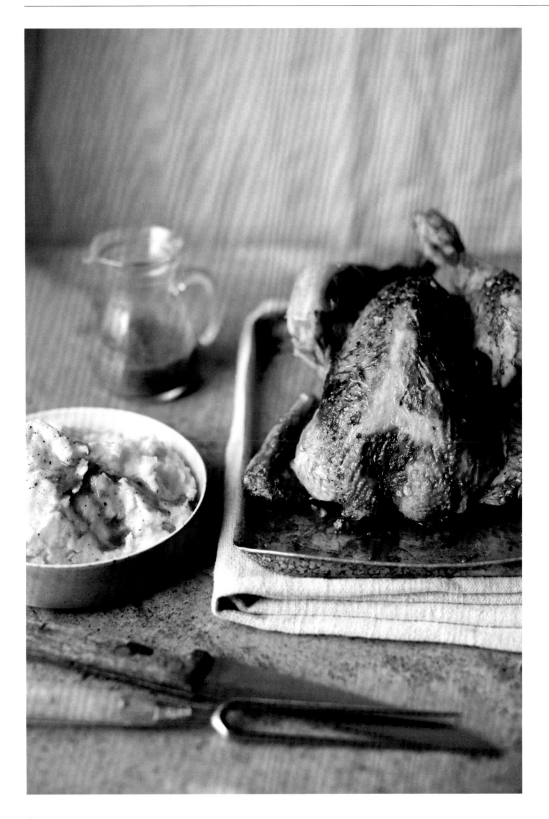

# Roasted Chicken with Parsnip and Potato Mash

*There are few things more comforting or simple than a roasted chicken — it's a guaranteed crowd pleaser. Before it's even ready, the delicious smell wafting from the oven will have your family gathering in the kitchen and salivating.*

**serves 4**

1 whole chicken (approx. 1.5kg/3lb 5oz)
1 lemon, halved
2 garlic cloves, halved
1 thyme or rosemary sprig
50g (1¾oz) butter, softened
½ shallot, finely chopped

300ml (10fl oz) chicken stock
salt and freshly ground black pepper

**For the mash:**
500g (1lb 2oz) potatoes, peeled and chopped into bite-sized pieces

400g (14oz) parsnips, peeled and chopped into bite-sized pieces
1 teaspoon salt
175ml (6fl oz) whole milk, warmed
30g (1oz) butter, cubed

Preheat the oven to 200°C (400°F), Gas Mark 6.

Remove the string from the chicken and stuff it with the lemon, garlic and herbs. Lay the chicken in a large roasting pan and, using your hands, rub the butter all over its skin. Season generously with salt and pepper and transfer to the oven to bake for around 50 minutes, until the juices run clear and the internal temperature of the meat is 65–70°C (150–160°F). Remove the lemon, garlic and herbs from the chicken and set aside in a medium pan to rest, covered, for at least 20 minutes.

While the chicken is cooling, prepare the mash. Place the potatoes and parsnips in a large pan and cover with water. Add the salt to the pan and place over a high heat. Once boiling, reduce the heat to a simmer and leave to cook for 20–25 minutes, until the vegetables are tender. Drain through a colander and return the vegetables to the pan. Using a potato masher, mash the vegetables to the consistency that you like, gradually adding the milk and butter as you go. Season to taste and transfer to a serving dish and season with black pepper. Keep warm while you prepare the sauce.

Place the pan with the reserved lemon, garlic and herbs over a low heat and squeeze the lemons to release the juice. Discard the lemon halves and add the shallot to the pan. Cook for 5 minutes, until the shallot is softened, then add the chicken stock along with any juices that have oozed out of the chicken. Bring to a simmer and leave to cook for 5–10 minutes, until reduced by half and thickened.

Carve the chicken and serve with the mash and sauce alongside.

# Butternut Pancakes

*The butternut squash used in these pancakes imparts a delicious natural sweetness. These are perfect served as they are, but can be paired with a simple salad for a more substantial meal.*

**serves 4**

400g (14oz) butternut
  squash, peeled and seeds
  removed, roughly chopped
2 eggs
125ml (4½fl oz) Greek
  yogurt
25g (1oz) butter, melted
70g (2½oz) plain flour
1 pinch of ground nutmeg

1 tablespoon olive oil
salt and freshly ground
  black pepper

Preheat the oven to 160°C (325°F), Gas Mark 3 and line a large baking sheet with greaseproof paper.

Lay the butternut squash out on the prepared baking sheet in a single layer and transfer to the oven to cook for 25 minutes, until tender. Once cooked through, transfer the pieces of squash to a large bowl and mash with a fork to obtain a rough purée.

In a separate bowl, whisk together the eggs, yogurt and melted butter until well combined. Add the butternut purée and sift in the flour. Add the nutmeg and season with salt and pepper, then whisk the mixture until well combined. Cover with clingfilm and transfer to the fridge to rest for 30 minutes.

Once the mixture has rested, heat the oil in a frying pan over a medium heat. Once hot, pour a small ladleful of the mixture into the pan. Cook the pancake for 2 minutes, then flip and cook for 2 minutes more, until just golden brown. Keep warm while you make the remaining pancakes.

Serve the pancakes warm, paired with a simple salad, if liked.

# Lapin à la Moutarde

*This is a traditional braised rabbit recipe that is enjoyed by families all over France. The sauce is deliciously rich and creamy but is given a fiery punch by the combination of mustards used.*

**serves 4**

1 whole rabbit, jointed or unjointed
2 tablespoons wholegrain mustard
50g (1¾oz) butter
1 onion, finely chopped

1 carrot, peeled and diced into 1cm (½ inch) cubes
100g mushrooms, roughly chopped
1 garlic clove, crushed
1 thyme sprig
300ml (½ pint) dry white wine

400ml (14fl oz) chicken stock
2 teaspoons Dijon mustard
200ml (7fl oz) double cream
½ bunch of flat-leaf parsley, leaves chopped
salt and freshly ground black pepper

If jointing your rabbit yourself, take the rabbit carcass and lay it on its back. Start by removing the hind legs with a sharp knife, following the hip joint. Next, make an incision between the rib cage and the saddle and dislocate one from the other with your hands. Finally, remove the front legs, slicing through the collar bone. You should be left with 6 joints of rabbit.

Preheat the oven to 160°C (325°F), Gas Mark 3.

Place the rabbit pieces in a large bowl and smear with 1 tablespoon of the wholegrain mustard. Season with salt and pepper and set aside.

Place the butter in a large flameproof casserole dish over a medium heat. Once it is melted and bubbling, add the pieces of rabbit and sear until just golden on all sides, then remove from the pan and set aside. In the same pan, add the onion, carrot, mushrooms, garlic and thyme sprig and cook, stirring continuously, for about 10 minutes, until the vegetables are just tender.

Deglaze the pan with the white wine and continue to cook until almost all of the alcohol has evaporated. Add the chicken stock, Dijon mustard and remaining wholegrain mustard, stir to combine, then return the rabbit pieces to the pan. Cover the pan with a lid and transfer to the oven to cook for about 25 minutes, until the rabbit is tender.

Pour the cream into the sauce, sprinkle over the chopped parsley and season to taste. Remove the pieces of rabbit from the pan and divide between serving plates, spooning over the sauce. Serve hot.

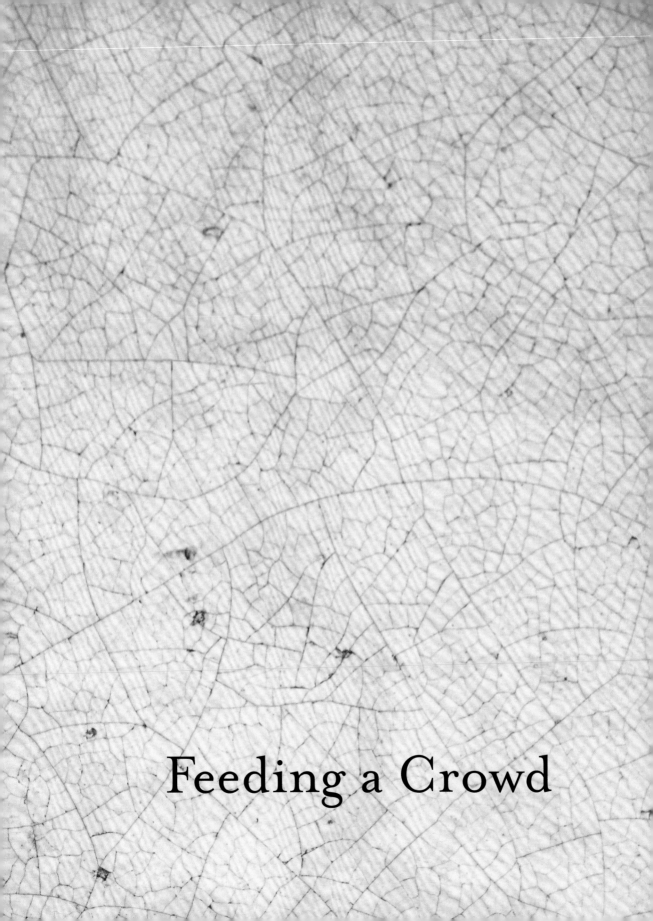

# Feeding a Crowd

## Giselle

When family or friends are coming over we like
to prepare as much of the food as possible in
advance so we can enjoy ourselves with our
guests. Many of these dishes are those that I ate
as a child, such as *Pissaladière* (*see* page 98)
and tarts. Both of these can be cut into bite-
sized pieces and eaten as an appetizer to whet
your appetite. We also make traditional southern
French dips such as Anchoïade and Tapenade (*see*
page 96), tripling the recipes for larger batches
that will fill several jars and serving them with
lots of crudités and good bread so that everyone
can help themselves. It's a very easy, relaxed
way to entertain and everyone from grandma to
young children loves finger food.

Another great treat is *Petites Fritures* (deep-
fried whitebait with tartare sauce; *see* page
114), which we all find irresistible. And then
there is our beautiful white pizza with a
topping of lardons, white onion, crème fraîche
and Roquefort (*see* page 102) – not a tomato in
sight. That also disappears extra fast.

All of the recipes in this chapter serve more
than four people as part of a larger spread.

# Spreads and Dips

*These are probably the easiest recipes to feed a crowd with. Not only are they super-tasty snacks, they only take a couple of minutes to make and they are typically provincial. They are perfect served on grilled bread or simply used as a dipping sauce.*

## Anchoïade

**makes 1 small jar, about 350g (12oz)**

60g (2¼oz) anchovy fillets from a jar
1 teaspoon small capers
1 garlic clove, peeled
1 teaspoon Dijon mustard
½ shallot, roughly chopped
1 tablespoon lemon juice
1 handful of parsley, chopped
1 pinch of freshly ground black pepper
4 tablespoons good-quality olive oil

Place all the ingredients, except the oil, in a small processor and blitz for a few seconds before gently adding the oil in a steady stream until the sauce has emulsified and thickened. Store in a sealed sterilized jar in the fridge for up to 10 days.

## Tapenade

**makes 1 small jar, about 350g (12oz)**

250g (9oz) pitted black olives
6 anchovy fillets from a jar
2 tablespoons small capers
1 garlic clove, peeled
100ml (3½fl oz) olive oil

Place all the ingredients, except the oil, in a small food processor and blitz together for a few seconds before gently adding the olive oil in a steady stream until thickened. Store in a sealed sterilized jar in the fridge for up to 10 days.

## *Brandade de Morue*

**serves 6 as an aperitif**

300g (10½oz) dried, salted stock fish
  fillets (unsalted fish, such as cod,
  which is air- and wind-dried on
  wooden racks)
150ml (¼ pint) warm milk
150ml (¼ pint) good-quality olive oil
freshly ground black pepper

Soak the fish for 48 hours in cold water, changing it every 12 hours. Once the time is completed, drain and place the fillets in a large saucepan and pour in enough fresh cold water to cover. Cook over a medium heat and, as soon as the water has reached boiling point, turn off the heat and leave the fish to poach for 10 minutes. Remove the fish from the pan and flake the flesh, making sure you remove any bones. Do not remove the skin, as this helps bind the spread.

For an authentic brandade, place the cooked fish in a mortar, add pepper to taste and grind with a pestle until it is a paste-like texture. Place in a cast-iron pan over a low heat and reheat, then while stirring vigorously, alternately pour in a little milk and olive oil. Continue until both liquids have been completely combined, without ever simmering or boiling. Leave to cool, then serve cold. Store in an airtight container in the fridge for 3–4 days.

# *Pissaladière*

*This is a typical southern French recipe, full of audacious flavours
and perfect to slice into bite-sized morsels to feed guests.*

**serves 4**

2 tablespoons olive oil
1kg (2lb 4oz) white onions
  (or 5 large pieces),
  finely sliced
20g (¾oz) chopped salted
  anchovies
30g (1oz) Anchoïade or
  Tapenade (*see* page 96)
1 thyme sprig

1 sheet of puff pastry
  (approx. 400g/14oz)
1 egg yolk mixed with
  1 tablespoon milk to use
  as an egg wash
6 fresh or lightly smoked
  anchovies
freshly ground black
  pepper
green salad, to serve
  (optional)

Preheat the oven to 180°C (350°F), Gas Mark 4.

Heat the oil in a large saucepan, then add the onions and sear over a high heat for at least 5 minutes, stirring constantly. Once the onions start to colour and tenderize, reduce the heat and add the salted anchovies together with the Anchoïade or Tapenade and thyme. Cover the pan with a lid and leave the onions to cook gently for a further hour, stirring every 10 minutes. Once the onions have reduced by half and are a beautiful caramelized colour, uncover and cook for another 10 minutes. All the moisture left in the saucepan will evaporate, leaving you with a delicious onion paste. Season with a pinch of pepper before leaving to cool completely.

Place the puff pastry on a baking sheet and prick all over with a fork. Fold over the edges to create a crust and brush all over with the egg wash. Precook the puff pastry in the oven for 7 minutes (this ensures that it won't get a soggy base). Spread the onion mixture all over the part-cooked pastry, staying within the crust. Once again, brush the edges of the pastry with egg wash for extra shininess. Bake in the oven for 30 minutes, or until the pastry is golden brown and crisp.

Remove from the oven and scatter the fresh anchovies over the top. Best served lukewarm or cold with a lovely green salad.

# Roasted Onion, Fennel and Pesto Tart

*Giselle: This recipe is a huge favourite of all the family, especially my mother, who really enjoys eating this tart as a sophisticated appetizer.*

**makes a 25cm (10 inch) tart**

2 tablespoons butter,
  plus a little extra
  for greasing
6 red onions, quartered
3 large fennel bulbs,
  halved
1 drizzle of olive oil
1 thyme sprig
15g (½oz) caster sugar

2 egg yolks, beaten, to
  make an egg wash
3 tablespoons basil pesto
10g (¼oz) toasted pine
  nuts
10g (¼oz) Parmesan
  shavings
1 handful of basil leaves
  (optional)
salt and freshly ground
  black pepper

**For the shortcrust pastry:**
225g (8oz) plain flour,
  plus extra for dusting
1 teaspoon salt
25g (1oz) cold butter,
  cubed
25g (1oz) lard, cubed
2 tablespoons cold water

To make the pastry, sift the flour and salt into a large bowl. Add the butter and lard and rub together with your fingertips until the mixture resembles breadcrumbs. Pour in the water and bring the dough together in your hands; but do not overwork it. Leave to rest in the fridge for 30 minutes before using.

Preheat the oven to 180°C (350°F), Gas Mark 4. Line a large baking tray with foil and grease a 25cm (10 inch) tart tin with butter.

Place the chopped onions and fennel on the prepared baking tray and drizzle the oil over the top. Season with salt and pepper, add the thyme, then mix together. Bake in the oven for 25 minutes, or until the veggies start to brown on the edges but are not completely cooked. Keep the oven on.

Heat the butter in a large frying pan over a medium heat, then scatter the sugar into the pan. Throw in the vegetable chunks and mix around for 2–3 minutes until they are coated with a light caramel, then remove from the pan and leave to cool.

Roll out the pastry on a lightly floured surface until 5mm (¼ inch) thick and use to line the prepared tart tin. Press the pastry into place before trimming off any excess pastry around the edges. Prick the base of the tart with a fork and brush all over with the beaten egg yolks. Blind bake in the oven for 20 minutes, then remove the tart, remove the baking beans, and carefully take the tart out of the tin. Leave to cool until the pastry is cool enough to handle.

Elegantly arrange the roasted onions and fennel in the pastry case then dollop the pesto in the spaces in between. Brush the rims again with the remaining egg wash and bake the tart in the oven for a further 10–15 minutes. Once all the vegetables are roasted and the pastry is brown, remove from the oven and sprinkle the pine nuts and Parmesan shavings on top while the tart is still warm. Serve with basil leaves scattered over the top, if liked.

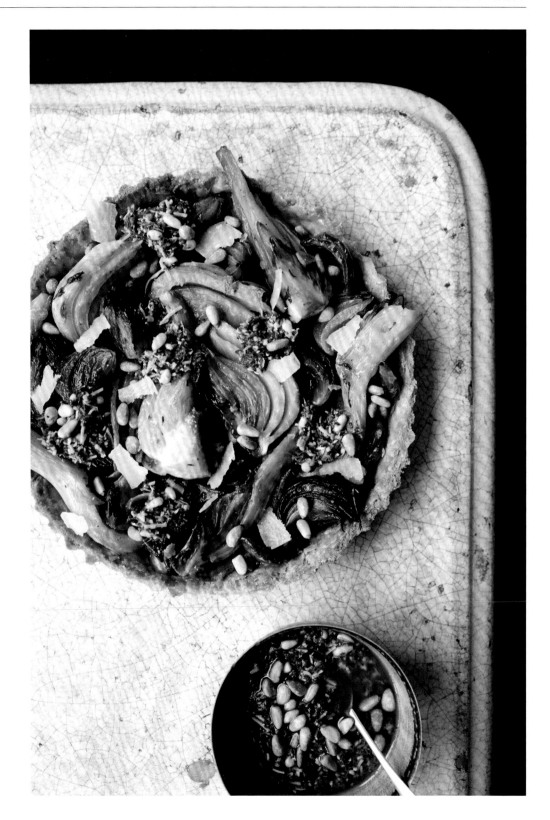

# White Pizza with Lardons and Crème Fraîche

*Tomato sauce–less pizzas are delicious; just be sure to pack in the bold flavours with the topping.*

**makes 1 × 30cm (12 inch) pizza**

2 tablespoons olive oil
1 large white onion,
  finely sliced
1 teaspoon dried mixed
  herbs
200g (7oz) smoked bacon
  lardons

250g (9oz) Pizza Dough
  (*see* page 242)
plain flour, for dusting
100g (3½oz) crème fraîche
30g (1oz) Roquefort
  cheese, cut into small
  pieces
salt and freshly ground
  black pepper

Line a large baking tray with greaseproof paper.

Heat the oil in a large saucepan over a medium heat. Add the sliced onions and cook for 5 minutes, stirring occasionally. Season with salt, pepper and the dried mixed herbs. Once the onions are tender, remove them from the pan and set aside on kitchen paper.

Dry-fry the lardons in a nonstick frying pan over a medium–high heat. Once they have rendered their water and begin to colour, immediately remove them from the heat.

Roll out the pizza dough on a lightly floured surface to the size of the baking tray and slide it onto the prepared baking tray. Spread the crème fraîche over the dough and scatter the cooked lardons and onions on top. Bake in the oven for 15–20 minutes until brown and crispy on the outside. Remove from the oven and sprinkle the Roquefort all over to melt, and season with pepper.

# Spinach and Goats' Cheese Quiche

*If you like goats' cheese, this recipe is perfect for you. It is a crispy and creamy heavenliness.*

**makes a 25cm (10 inch) quiche**

1 tablespoon butter
2 garlic cloves, chopped
600g (1lb 5oz) spinach
  leaves, tough stems
  removed
250g (9oz) rolled-out
  puff pastry
1 egg yolk mixed with
  1 tablespoon milk to
  use as an egg wash

3 whole eggs
100ml (3½fl oz) semi-
  skimmed milk
80ml (2¾fl oz) double cream
100g (3½oz) soft goats'
  cheese, cut into
  bite-sized pieces
salt and freshly ground
  black pepper

Heat the butter in a saucepan with the chopped garlic. When the garlic is beginning to brown, after about 2 minutes, add the spinach leaves. Use a spatula to make sure all the leaves get coated in butter and garlic and season to taste with salt and pepper. Cover the pan with a lid and cook for 3 minutes until the spinach has completely wilted. Remove from the heat and drain. Firmly press the spinach in a colander with the back of a spoon to remove any excess water. Leave the cooked spinach to cool in the fridge for 2 hours before roughly chopping with a sharp knife.

Preheat the oven to 180°C (350°F), Gas Mark 4.

Line a 25cm (10 inch) quiche tin with the puff pastry, then brush the pastry with egg wash. Make a few little incisions with help of a fork and blind bake the puff pastry in the oven for 15 minutes to prevent the base going soggy. As soon as the pastry is lightly blond, remove from the oven, remove the baking beans and evenly spread out the chopped spinach over the pastry.

Whisk the eggs, milk and double cream together in a medium bowl and season with salt and pepper. Pour the mixture over the spinach to cover (the mix will rise during cooking). Finally, scatter the goats' cheese over the quiche and bake in the oven for 40 minutes until lovely and golden. Best served lukewarm or cold.

# Meat Loaf

*This is real sharing comfort food!*

**serves 4**

½ carrot, chopped
½ celery stick, chopped
2 white mushrooms, chopped
1 shallot, chopped
2 garlic cloves
1 handful of flat-leaf
  parsley leaves
450g (1lb) minced beef
3 tablespoons panko
  (Japanese breadcrumbs)
1 teaspoon dried thyme

2 teaspoons fine salt
1 pinch of ground nutmeg
1 pinch of dried red
  chilli flakes
1 egg
2 tablespoons ketchup,
  plus a little extra
  for brushing
1 tablespoon
  Worcestershire sauce

Preheat the oven to 190°C (375°F), Gas Mark 5.

Place the carrot, celery, mushroom and shallot together with the garlic and parsley in a small blender and lightly blitz into small chunks; being careful not to purée the vegetables. Set aside.

Place the minced meat in a large bowl, add the breadcrumbs and thyme, then season with the salt, nutmeg and chilli. In a separate smaller bowl, whisk the egg, ketchup and Worcestershire sauce together before adding to the minced meat. Finally, add the chopped veggies and gently fold into the meat.

Shape the mixture into a 20cm (8 inch) long loaf on a baking tray lined with greaseproof paper, avoiding pressing and compacting the mixture, then brush a little ketchup on top of the meat loaf before baking. Alternatively, cook it in a loaf tin to retain its shape. Bake in the oven for approximately 30 minutes depending on the thickness of the minced meat, until it has a golden brown exterior and the centre has reached 65°C (149°F).

Remove the meat loaf from the oven and leave to rest for 2 hours before attempting to slice. It is delicious served cold as finger food.

# Spring Lamb Chops with Garlic and Mint Sauce

*We don't eat a lot of meat but this particular sharing dish is always welcomed come spring.*

**serves 4 as an aperitif**

1 rack of spring lamb
  (with 8 bones), French
  trimmed

**For the marinade:**
4 tablespoons olive oil
1 rosemary sprig, leaves
  picked

1 thyme sprig, leaves
  picked
1 teaspoon *piment
  d'Espelette* or chilli
  powder
1 teaspoon sea salt

**For the sauce:**
100ml (3½fl oz) milk
2 garlic cloves, halved

250ml (9fl oz) rapeseed oil
1 tablespoon chopped mint
1 tablespoon chopped
  flat-leaf parsley
salt and freshly ground
  black pepper

For the marinade, place all the ingredients in a mortar and grind with a pestle until the oil is properly incorporated. Rub the marinade all over the lamb rack and leave in the fridge for 4 hours.

To make the sauce, place the milk and garlic in a small saucepan and gently heat making sure the liquid never boils. Once hot, use a hand-held blender to mix the garlic and milk together, then gradually incorporate the oil into the mixture until the sauce emulsifies and thickens. Season to taste, pour the sauce into a small bowl and leave to cool for 1 hour. Once completely cold, whisk the chopped herbs into the sauce.

Preheat the oven to 180°C (350°F), Gas Mark 4.

Season the rack of lamb to taste with salt and pepper. Heat a large frying pan over a medium–high heat and brown the rack on the meaty sides for about 1–2 minutes, then turn over and colour the other sides for a further 1 minute. Finally, brown the ends briefly so that all of the exposed meat is seared.

Place the rack in an appropriately sized roasting tray and roast in the oven for approximately 10 minutes depending on the size of the rack, or until the probe of a meat thermometer inserted into the core shows approximately 43°C/109°F. Leave the meat to rest for a further 5 minutes before slicing each chop and serving with the sauce.

# Pommes Dauphines

*These are a thousand times more delicious than crisps. Make your own scrumptious* pommes dauphines *to accompany your dipping sauces (see page 96). It is preferable to make the mixture the day before.*

**makes 30–40, depending on size**

800g (1lb 12oz) potatoes,
  peeled and quartered
1 teaspoon grated nutmeg
1 teaspoon fine salt
1 pinch of freshly ground
  black pepper
approx. 1 litre vegetable
  oil, for frying

**For the choux pastry:**

120g (4¼oz) plain flour
a good pinch of sea salt
250ml (9fl oz) whole or
  semi-skimmed milk
90g (3¼oz) butter
4 eggs

Place the potatoes in a saucepan filled with cold salted water and cook for 15–20 minutes until tender.

Meanwhile, it is important that you prepare the choux pastry in advance, as both elements must still be warm when they are mixed together. Sift the flour and salt into bowl and set aside. Put the milk and butter in a medium saucepan over a medium heat and stir until the butter melts. Allow the mixture to come to a rolling boil, then immediately remove the pan from the heat. Add the flour and salt to the saucepan in one go and mix well with a wooden spoon until it all comes together as a dough. Reduce the heat to a minimum and keep stirring the dough energetically for a further 2 minutes (it's normal that the pastry starts sticking to the base of the pan). Place the dough in a large bowl and vigorously beat the eggs in, one by one. You should have a smooth choux pastry.

As soon as the potatoes are cooked, drain thoroughly and pass through a potato ricer. Weigh out 500g (1lb 2oz) and add to the choux pastry. Mix well with a wooden spoon and season well with nutmeg, salt and pepper. Leave in the fridge overnight.

The next day, heat a deep-fryer or shallow pan with vegetable oil to 180°C (350°F).

Scoop out 1 tablespoon of the mix and gently add spoonfuls to the hot oil. Fry them for 2 minutes until golden brown and crispy, then remove with a slotted spoon and drain on kitchen paper. Serve immediately.

# Salmon Fish Cakes

*We absolutely love this recipe — delicious fish cakes bursting with herby flavours.*

**makes 5 small fish cakes**

150g (5½oz) salmon fillets,
  scaled and pin-boned
200ml (7fl oz) whole or
  semi-skimmed milk
1 thyme sprig
130g (4½oz) mashed potato
  (about 2 large potatoes)
1 tablespoon olive oil
1 egg

30g (1oz) breadcrumbs
  (either panko or dried)
5g (⅛ oz) chopped
  coriander
5g (⅛oz) chopped chives
finely grated zest of
  ½ lime
4 tablespoons avocado or
  coconut oil, for frying
salt and freshly ground
  black pepper

mixed salad leaves,
  to garnish

**For the coating:**
about 75g (2¾oz) plain
  flour
2 eggs
100g (3½oz) dried
  breadcrumbs

Place the fish in a saucepan and pour over the milk. Add a pinch of salt and the thyme before gently bringing to the boil. As soon as the first big bubbles appear turn off the heat and set aside. Once the milk is lukewarm remove the fish and flake the flesh. Set aside.

In a large bowl, add all the remaining ingredients in no particular order including the flaked salmon. Season to taste and mix together until combined, then leave to set in the fridge for 2 hours. Once chilled, divide the fish cake mixture into 5 portions, then shape and pat into circles about 2cm (¾ inch) thick (as you would when making a burger).

All the ingredients needed for the coating must be put in individual shallow dishes. The eggs must be beaten and seasoned with a pinch of salt and pepper before using.

Bring the avocado oil to a medium heat or 180°C (350°F) in a large pan. Meanwhile, coat the fish cakes in the flour, shaking off the excess, then repeat the process with the beaten eggs, letting the excess drip off. Finally, dredge the fish cakes in breadcrumbs, turning twice and patting to adhere.

Pan-sear the fish cakes, in batches, for 2 minutes on each side until a caramelized brown colour, then remove and drain on kitchen paper. Garnish with mixed salad leaves and serve immediately.

# *Petites Fritures*

*We generally buy whitebait from our local market. They are extremely easy to prepare
and, deep-fried and served with tartare sauce, are perfect to feed a hungry crowd.*

**serves 4 as finger food**

500g (1lb 2oz) whitebait
1 teaspoon salt, plus a
  pinch
65g (2¼oz) plain flour
rapeseed or sunflower oil,
  for frying

**For the tartare sauce:**
1 large egg yolk
1 teaspoon Dijon mustard
2 tablespoons lemon juice
150ml (¼ pint) sunflower
  or rapeseed oil
½ shallot, finely chopped
1 tablespoon chopped
  capers

1 tablespoon chopped
  gherkins
1 handful of curly
  parsley, chopped
1 teaspoon white wine
  vinegar (optional)
salt and freshly ground
  black pepper

Heat the oil in a deep-fryer to 180°C (350°F).

For the sauce, place the egg yolk, mustard and 1 tablespoon of the lemon juice in a small bowl. While whisking, gradually incorporate half of the oil until the sauce thickens and emulsifies like a mayonnaise. Whisk in the remaining lemon juice and oil until combined. Rinse the shallot under cold water then add to the mayonnaise with the capers, gherkins and chopped parsley and mix until combined. Season well with salt, pepper and the vinegar if needed.

Rinse the small fish under cold water making sure no impurities remain, then pat dry with kitchen paper before covering the fish with the 1 teaspoon salt and the flour. Use your hands to mix and fully coat the whitebait in the flour.

If you don't have a fryer, heat the oil in a deep frying pan to 180°C (350°F). Fry the fish in several batches for 3–5 minutes until golden brown and crispy. Remove with a slotted spoon and drain on kitchen paper. Sprinkle a pinch of salt on the whitebait as soon as you remove them from the pan and serve piping hot with the tartare sauce.

# Wild Mushroom Bruschetta

*Giselle: My siblings and I used to compete in mushroom picking as children, especially in spring when our favourite varieties were out.*

**serves 4**

300g (10½oz) wild
  mushrooms, such as
  St George, mousseron
  and oyster
2 tablespoons olive oil,
  plus extra for drizzling
1 shallot, finely chopped
1 tablespoon butter

1 garlic clove, halved
4 thick slices of
  sourdough
1 handful of watercress
30g (1oz) Parmesan
  shavings
salt and freshly ground
  black pepper

Brush any grit off the mushrooms and slice them until they are all the same size.

Heat the olive oil in a large frying pan and cook the mushrooms over a medium–high heat for 2 minutes until wilted. Add the shallot to the pan together with the butter and stir with a fork pricked with a garlic half. Season to taste with salt and pepper.

Remove the mushrooms from the pan once they are crisp and lightly browned.

Meanwhile, heat a chargrill pan over a medium–high heat. Brush the bread on both sides with a drizzle of oil, then toast on the chargrill for 2 minutes each side or until lightly charred. Rub one side with the remaining garlic clove.

Stir the watercress leaves into the mushroom mixture and immediately pile onto the toasted bread. Finish with the Parmesan shavings.

# 'Honeycomb' Courgette Cannelloni

*This baked dish is as visually appealing as it is tasty!*

**serves 3–4 and fills a 20cm (8 inch) round ovenproof dish**

3 large courgettes
  (500g/11b 2oz)
salt and freshly ground
  black pepper

**For the lamb filling:**
1 tablespoon olive oil
2 garlic cloves, finely
  chopped
1 shallot, finely chopped
200g (7oz) brown button
  mushrooms, chopped or
  pulsed several times
  in a blender
200g (7oz) minced lamb
1 tablespoon chopped thyme
150g (5½oz) spreadable
  soft goats' cheese

**For the béchamel:**
35g (1¼oz) butter
35g (1¼oz) plain flour
280ml (9½fl oz) milk
30g (1oz) grated Beaufort
  or Gruyère cheese, plus
  a little extra for
  topping
2-3 pinches of ground
  nutmeg, to taste

For the filling, heat the olive oil in a frying pan over a medium heat. Add the garlic and shallots and sauté for 2 minutes until translucent. Add the chopped mushrooms and season well. Once the mushrooms have rendered all their water, transfer them to a bowl. Use the same frying pan to sauté the minced meat. Cook for 3–4 minutes until slightly coloured and cooked through. Season with salt, pepper and thyme before adding to the bowl with the mushrooms. While still hot, incorporate the soft goats' cheese. Once it is melted the mixture should have a perfectly moist texture. Set aside.

Finely slice the courgettes with a mandolin or a knife approximately 5mm (¼ inch) thick. The courgette strips must be thin enough to manipulate, but thick enough to remain stable in the dish. Bring a large pot of salted water to the boil and add all the courgette strips. After 1½ minutes, drain the courgettes and immediately refresh in a bowl of ice-cold water. Make sure the strips are patted dry with kitchen paper before using. Roll up

each courgette strip and tightly place them in a 20cm (8 inch) round ovenproof dish to create a 'honeycomb' bed of greenery. Fill three-quarters of each hole with the lamb filling, making sure you press the meat down to get enough in each courgette.

Preheat the oven to 180°C (350°F), Gas Mark 4.

To make the béchamel, place the butter in a medium saucepan and melt. Add the flour to the pan and whisk together until it is a thick homogenous paste (known as a 'roux'). Gradually incorporate the milk, whisking constantly so no lumps form. Boil for 2 minutes until thick and glossy. Finally, add the cheese and season well with salt, pepper and nutmeg.

While the béchamel is still hot and malleable, delicately spoon over the remaining meat to top up the courgette tubes. You should have a beautiful dish resembling honeycomb. Sprinkle with more cheese over the top and bake in the oven for 20–25 minutes until the béchamel has crisped and coloured. Serve immediately.

# Truffled Camembert

*The Ardèche is known for its fragrant truffles, so make sure to use them in your favourite dishes. The whole Roux family are cheese lovers, and on special occasions this particular recipe sits more than happily on the cheese board.*

**serves 4**

100g (3½oz) good-quality
  mascarpone
80g (3oz) cooked and
  peeled chestnuts
35g (1¼oz) fresh black
  truffle
1 Camembert cheese
  (250g/9oz), chilled
salt and freshly ground
  black pepper

Whisk the mascarpone to a creamy consistency in a large bowl. Roughly chop the chestnuts and finely grate the truffle before adding both to the bowl. Mix and season to taste with salt and pepper.

Delicately slice the refrigerated Camembert cheese in half horizontally and spread the mascarpone mixture onto one inside. Put the other half of the cheese on top to close, then wrap in clingfilm. Leave in the refrigerator for 48 hours. For extra flavour and creaminess remember to take out the truffled cheese at least 2 hours before serving.

# Spinach, Red Onion and Blue Cheese Bread Pudding

*This is the ideal recipe when you have a few slices of stale bread in your cupboard. Economic, utterly delicious and an original twist on a classic dessert that everybody enjoys.*

**serves 4**

1 tablespoon butter, plus
  extra for greasing
4 red onions, finely sliced
2 tablespoons cider
  vinegar
500g (1lb 2oz) spinach
1 garlic clove, smashed
  with the palm of your
  hand

2 tablespoons Dijon grain
  mustard
2 eggs
200ml (7fl oz) whole milk
100g (3½oz) crème fraîche
1 pinch of ground nutmeg
7-8 slices of bloomer bread
75g (2¾oz) blue cheese,
  such as Stilton
salt and freshly ground
  black pepper

Preheat the oven to 180°C (350°F), Gas Mark 4 and grease a 22cm (8½ inch) round cake tin with butter.

Heat ½ tablespoon of the butter in a large frying pan over a medium–high heat before adding the onions. Once they have rendered all their water, deglaze with the cider vinegar and reduce the heat. Cook the onions for 15–20 minutes, stirring occasionally, until soft and a beautiful caramel colour. Season to taste with salt and pepper and leave to cool.

Cut off the thick stems of the spinach and thoroughly rinse the leaves under cold running water to remove any sand or dirt. Drain and place in a salad spinner to remove any excess water.

Heat the remaining butter in a large frying pan over a medium–high heat. Add the crushed garlic to the pan followed by the spinach and sauté for 3 minutes until the spinach is completely wilted and there is no liquid left in the pan. Season to taste, then remove and discard the garlic and take the pan off the heat.

Whisk the mustard and eggs together in a large bowl. Gradually pour in the milk and crème fraîche, then season with salt, pepper and nutmeg. Place the sliced bread into the egg mixture and leave for 2 minutes to absorb enough liquid without going soggy and unmalleable.

Delicately fill the base of your greased mould by arranging 2 large slices of bread on the bottom. Place the cooked spinach, onions and remaining bread on top, then pour any of the remaining liquid mixture into the dish to fill all the little nooks and crannies. Finally, crumble over the blue cheese and bake in the oven for 15–20 minutes until golden brown and crispy. Serve immediately.

# Today's Trends

# Emily

I've been lucky as I have grown up around good food, travelled to many countries and eaten in so many nice places. I have also worked in some amazing restaurants and now I'm developing my own style of cooking. I'm interested in the trends of today but I like to use them in the way that I want to eat. I like lighter food than the traditional French style. My aim is to take the trends but make them yummier while keeping the food healthy. I love ingredients like kale, sprouting broccoli, red rice and avocado, all of which are so good for you but also delicious. I don't drink coffee but I find it very interesting to cook with as I love the flavour.

I wasn't really aware of all these food trends when I was working in Paris - the French are just not into them like we are in Britain. But when I came home I found that mum had things like quinoa and coconut flour in her cupboard - she's always been keen on the latest ideas and on healthy ingredients - and I began to cook with them. The recipes I've come up with take a modern approach. They don't contain much fat or sugar, and there are few sauces, but there is lots of flavour. I enjoy reinterpreting classic French techniques in a way that appeals to younger people today, and working with unusual ingredients, such as kabocha squash and chia seeds. I also like to experiment with gluten-free dishes, and everyone enjoys the recipe for Gluten- and Dairy-free Blueberry and Hazelnut Muffins (see page 130) that mum shared with me.

# Dairy-free Avocado Mousse and Gluten-free Granola

*Emily: Avocado is a huge favourite of mine; I use it as much in sweet as in savoury dishes. This is a really simple recipe that you can rustle up when there is a ripe avocado left in the fridge. Eat it as is just like yogurt, although, adding a little crunch with the granola makes the dessert even yummier.*

**mousse serves 3 and granola serves 4–6**

**For the granola:**
250g (9oz) gluten-free oats
60g (2¼oz) sunflower seeds
60g (2¼oz) pumpkin seeds
2 tablespoons linseeds
60g (2¼oz) hazelnuts, roughly chopped
40g (1½oz) flaked almonds
1 tablespoon coconut oil
65g (2¼oz) peanut butter
60g (2¼oz) honey
3 tablespoons maple syrup
65g (2¼oz) raisins
65g (2¼oz) goji berries

**For the mousse:**
2 avocados
40g (1½oz) unsweetened coconut milk or almond milk
40g (1½oz) honey
1 vanilla pod, scraped
2 tablespoons lemon juice

Preheat the oven to 120°C (250°F), Gas Mark ½ and line a baking tray with greaseproof paper.

Mix the oats, seeds and nuts together in a large bowl.

Place the oil, peanut butter, honey and maple syrup in a small saucepan and gently heat. Once all the ingredients are properly combined and melted pour over the dry mix. Make sure all the oats and nuts are coated before spreading out on the prepared baking tray. Bake in the oven for 1½ hours until beautifully golden brown, making sure to mix and break up the pieces halfway through cooking. Remove from the oven and incorporate the dried fruit. Leave to cool.

To make the mousse, mix all the ingredients together in a food processor until silky smooth. Sprinkle the granola on top and eat straight away as the avocado has a tendency to discolour.

# Black Chia Porridge with Bamboo Crunch

*Chia seeds are trendy nowadays with their numerous health benefits, although they can be a little bland if not prepared properly and accompanied with the right ingredients. If you are always in a hurry in the morning, this super-healthy porridge pot is the answer. You can prepare a few batches in advance and add different toppings as you go.*

**fills a 125ml (4fl oz) jar**

**For the porridge:**
70g (2½oz) blackberries,
  plus extra for the
  topping
100ml (3½fl oz) unsweetened
  almond milk
1 tablespoon lemon juice
1 tablespoon honey
50g (1¾oz) chia seeds

**For the bamboo crunch:**
42g (1½oz) demerara sugar
75g (2¾oz) plain flour
1 pinch of salt
12g (¼oz) ground bamboo
  charcoal (optional, buy
  online or from health-
  food shops)
50g (1¾oz) soft butter

To make the porridge, place all the ingredients, except the chia seeds, in a small food processor and blitz until it is a beautiful dark purple colour. Pour the mixture into a small jar and mix in the chia seeds. Leave in the fridge overnight to let the chia seeds swell up and double in size.

Preheat the oven to 180°C (350°F), Gas Mark 4 and line a baking tray with greaseproof paper.

For the bamboo crunch, mix the sugar, flour, salt and charcoal together in a medium bowl. Add the butter and rub it into the flour mix using your fingertips until it resembles large crumbs. Evenly spread the crumbs out on the prepared baking tray and bake in the oven for 15 minutes. Don't forget them as you won't be able to judge on colour. Remove from the oven and leave to cool and crunch up. If making ahead of time store in an airtight container for up to 3 days.

The next morning, scatter fresh blackberries on top of the porridge together with a few crunchy bites before devouring.

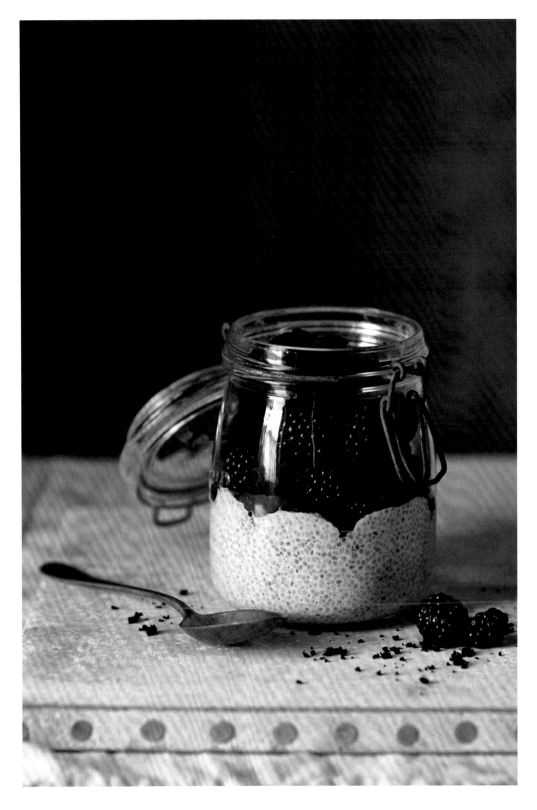

# Gluten- and Dairy-free Blueberry and Hazelnut Muffins

*Giselle: Michel and Emily usually find that gluten-free desserts don't quite satisfy them. However, this recipe has everybody's thumbs up!*

**makes about 12 large muffins**

120g (4¼oz) coconut flour
1 teaspoon bicarbonate
  of soda
½ teaspoon salt
200g (7oz) runny honey
200g (7oz) coconut milk

6 eggs
4 tablespoons melted
  coconut oil, plus a
  little extra for
  greasing
1 tablespoon vanilla
  extract

25g (1oz) chia seeds
50g (1¾oz) fresh
  blueberries
50g (1¾oz) hazelnuts,
  roughly chopped

Preheat the oven to 185°C (365°F), Gas Mark 4½ and lightly oil 12 muffin moulds or a 12-hole muffin tray.

Whisk the flour, bicarbonate of soda and salt together in a large bowl with a balloon whisk.

In a separate bowl, or blender, whisk the honey, milk, eggs, coconut oil and vanilla extract. Once everything is thoroughly combined pour over the dry mix and stir together until mixed. Finally, stir in the chia seeds, blueberries and hazelnuts. Stir for 2 minutes, as the chia seeds will absorb some of the moisture.

Fill the muffin moulds to just under the rim with the batter and bake in the oven for 20–25 minutes until golden brown and slightly risen. Leave to cool slightly before serving.

# Grilled Cobia, Garden Peas, Radishes and Black Butter

*Cobia is the new farmed sustainable fish on the market. Its firm white flesh is perfect for grilling, but if you can't find it use cod instead.*

**serves 4**

½ tablespoon butter
250g (9oz) garden peas
1 spring onion, finely
  sliced
480g (17oz) cobia or cod
  fillets (about 4 fillets)
olive oil, for drizzling
salt and freshly ground
  black pepper
microherbs, to garnish
  (optional)

**For the black butter:**
100ml (3½fl oz) white wine
  vinegar
130ml (4fl oz) white wine
2 shallots, roughly
  chopped
130g (4½oz) butter, cubed
2 sachets of squid ink

**For the roasted radishes:**
2 bunches of coloured
  radishes, halved or
  quartered so they are
  all the same size
  (reserve 1 or 2 raw)
1 tablespoon honey
2 tablespoons olive oil
1 tablespoon lemon juice

Preheat the oven to 220°C (425°F), Gas Mark 7.

To prepare the black butter, place the vinegar, wine and shallots in a medium saucepan and bring to a simmer. Cook for approximately 15 minutes, or until the shallots are tender and the liquid has reduced by two-thirds. Add the liquid and cooked shallots to a blender while still hot and blitz to a smooth paste. With the machine on, gradually add the cubed butter and squid ink, then season the glossy and thickened sauce.

For the roasted radishes, place the radishes in a large bowl together with the honey, olive oil, lemon juice and seasoning. Once all the radishes are properly coated, scatter them on a baking sheet and roast in the oven for 15–20 minutes, stirring frequently.

Heat the butter in a medium saucepan, add the fresh peas and sauté and season the peas for 2 minutes before adding the spring onion. Cover with a lid and cook for 5 minutes, or until the peas are tender.

Heat a griddle pan or barbecue to a medium–high heat. Season the cobia fillets with salt and pepper and drizzle a little olive oil on top. This fatty fish is best served pink, so depending on the size and thickness of the fish, cooking for 2 minutes on each side will suffice.

To serve, smear a tablespoon of the black butter on one side of each plate and place a grilled fish fillet on top. Arrange the peas and radishes elegantly on the side and garnish with microherbs, if liked.

# Roasted Kale with Cannellini Beans and Chorizo

*Although kale is super-trendy, it is difficult to drink the veggies raw in juice! It's much better to cook them in a tasty ragout.*

**serves 3**

70g (2½oz) kale leaves, roughly chopped
2 tablespoons olive oil
finely grated zest of 1 lemon
175g (6oz) cooking chorizo
2 small white onions (approx. 65g/2¼oz), sliced

2 garlic cloves, sliced
125g (4½oz) cherry tomatoes, quartered
240g (8½oz) cannellini beans, drained and rinsed
1 thyme sprig
250ml (9fl oz) water
salt and freshly ground black pepper

Preheat the oven to 120°C (250°F), Gas Mark ½ and line a large baking tray with greaseproof paper.

Place the kale in a large bowl, add the oil and salt and pepper, toss the kale until it is lightly coated all over, then spread it out on the prepared baking tray. Bake in the oven for about 20 minutes, or until a little crispy on the edges but still tender in the middle. Remove from the oven and sprinkle with lemon zest. Set aside.

Cut the chorizo into large diagonal slices, about 2cm (¾ inch) wide, and sear in a large nonstick frying pan over a medium–high heat for 3 minutes on each side (no fat needed), until lightly coloured. Once cooked, remove the chorizo from the pan and set aside on kitchen paper. Use the fat left in the pan

from the chorizo to sear the sliced onions and garlic for 3 minutes until tender, before adding the tomatoes to the pan. Gently stir and cook for a further 5 minutes until the tomatoes have softened. Finally, add the cannellini beans, thyme and measured water, then reduce the heat to a gentle simmer and cook for a further 7 minutes.

Season to taste and remember to discard the sprig of thyme before serving with the roasted kale.

# Individual Summer Tartelettes with a Quinoa Crust

*These little tartelettes are ideal for people who have a wheat intolerance.*
*The combinations of fruit and veggies you can use are endless.*

**makes 5 tartelettes, each 10cm (4 inches) wide**

microherbs, mint leaves
  and beetroot cress,
  to garnish (optional)

**For the quinoa crust:**
rapeseed or sunflower oil,
  for greasing
300g (10½oz) quinoa

1 egg, beaten
salt and freshly ground
  black pepper

**For the filling:**
5 eggs
160g (5¼oz) garden peas
1 tablespoon butter
1 spring onion, finely
  sliced

1 small red chilli, finely
  sliced (optional)
150g (5½oz) baby spinach
1 tablespoon finely chopped
  mint leaves
1 handful of Tomberry
  tomatoes, halved or
  small cherry tomatoes,
  quartered
80g (3oz) feta

Preheat the oven to 180°C (350°F), Gas Mark 4 and grease 5 tartelette tins, 10cm (4 inches) wide, with oil.

Cook the quinoa as you usually would in either water or vegetable stock (*see* page 49). Drain well and leave to cool in a bowl to room temperature. When the quinoa is at room temperature, incorporate the beaten egg and season with salt and pepper. The quinoa should no longer be crumbly but rather compact and holding itself together. At this point, start filling the prepared tartelette tins by gently pressing the mixture into place. The crust must be at least 5mm (¼ inch) thick for it to hold during cooking.

Place the tartelettes in the oven for 12 minutes. Crack an egg into each small tart and return to the oven for a further 5 minutes. Once

the egg is completely cooked, remove the tartelettes from the oven and leave to cool for a few minutes before carefully removing the crusts from the tins.

Meanwhile, blanch the peas for 1 minute in a pan of boiling salted water before refreshing in ice-cold water. Set aside.

Place the butter in a medium saucepan over a gentle heat. Add the spring onion, peas and chilli and sauté for 2 minutes. Remove from the heat, scatter in the spinach leaves and chopped mint and season well. Arrange the beautiful veggies all around the yolk and add the halved tomatoes and cheese for an extra tang. Garnish with a mixture of microherbs, mint leaves and beetroot cress, if liked, and serve immediately.

# Pork Loin, Carrot 'Spaghetti', Roasted Parsnip and Coriander Condiment

*This original recipe is full of bold and fragrant flavours that tantalize your taste buds. The combination of Moroccan spice with the freshness of coriander and lime juice brings the whole dish together.*

**serves 4**

600g (1lb 5oz) pork loin
1 tablespoon olive oil
salt and freshly ground
  black pepper

**For the coriander condiment:**
2 bunches of coriander
2 tablespoons lime juice

4 tablespoons olive oil
1 teaspoon Dijon mustard
1 ice cube

**For the garnish:**
4 small parsnips, unpeeled
  but thoroughly washed
1 tablespoon honey
2 tablespoons olive oil

2 carrots, spiralized or
  cut into ribbons with a
  vegetable peeler
1 pinch of ras-el-hanout
2 tablespoons lemon juice
1 handful of mint cress
  or sliced mint leaves
  (optional)

Preheat the oven to 180°C (350°F), Gas Mark 4.

Cut the pork into 4 even pieces and season with salt and pepper on each side. Heat the oil in large frying pan over a medium heat. Sear each side for 4–5 minutes, depending on the thickness of the meat until a lovely caramelized colour. Set aside.

To make the coriander condiment, blend all the ingredients together in a small food processor. Once all the ingredients are properly combined and it is a smooth paste, season with a pinch of salt. Store in the fridge until ready to use.

To prepare the garnish, place the parsnips on a baking tray together with the honey and 1 tablespoon of the olive oil. Mix together to coat the parsnips, then season with salt and pepper. Bake in the oven for 15–20 minutes, depending on the size of your veggies, until golden brown.

Meanwhile, heat 1 tablespoon of the olive oil in a large frying pan over a high heat. Place the spiralized carrots in the sizzling pan and sprinkle them with the ras-el-hanout. The carrots will cook very rapidly, so stir them constantly until they have softened but still remain *al dente*. Deglaze them with the lemon juice and season to taste with salt and pepper.

To serve, place a dash of the coriander condiment on the side of the plate with a small spatula or spoon. Intertwine a small nest of carrot 'spaghetti' and place the parsnip next to it. Finally, add the pork, crispy side up, and garnish with mint cress, if liked. Eat the carrot swirled around your fork (as you would real spaghetti).

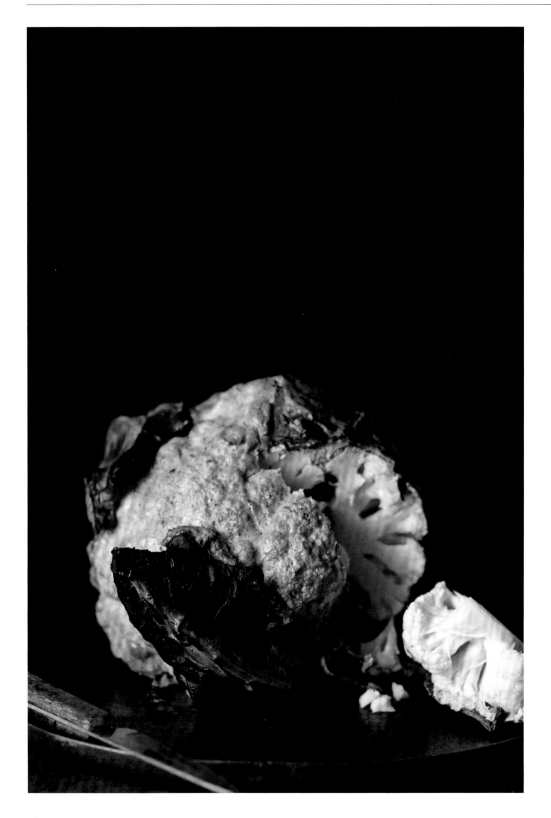

# Whole Roasted and Spiced Cauliflower

*This is an extremely easy recipe and perfect for a quick, light lunch. It's also a great vegetable accompaniment to Christmas lunch! You can always use the delicious yogurt topping to enlighten other dishes during the week.*

**serves 4–6**

150g (5½oz) Greek yogurt
finely grated zest and
  juice of 1 lemon
2 teaspoons smoked salt
1 tablespoon finely chopped
  garlic
1 tablespoon smoked
  paprika
1 teaspoon ground cumin
1 pinch of freshly ground
  black pepper
1 pinch of ground nutmeg
1 cauliflower head
good-quality olive oil,
  for drizzling

Preheat the oven to 200°C (400°F), Gas Mark 6 and line a baking tray with greaseproof paper.

Whisk all the ingredients, except for the cauliflower and olive oil, together in a large bowl. Dunk the whole cauliflower into the bowl and smear the marinade all over, then place it on the prepared baking tray. Bake in the oven for 45–60 minutes, or until the marinade has formed a beautifully coloured crust.

It is best served lukewarm with a drizzle of good-quality olive oil. If you have any remaining marinade sauce, then keep it to serve with any fish or meat.

# Spelt 'Risotto', Sprouting Broccoli and Ceps

*Spelt is a fantastic alternative to rice; it has a slightly nutty flavour and is very easily digested, especially for people who have difficulty digesting gluten. It also gives a warming and heartier feel to many dishes. Spelt is extremely versatile and can be used in many different ways. Here, spelt is used to make a wintery 'risotto', but it can be made into biscuits, breads and is also a great supplement to salads.*

**serves 4**

1 litre (1¾ pints)
  vegetable stock or water
3 tablespoons olive oil
1 white onion, finely diced
200g (7oz) pearled spelt
125ml (4fl oz) white wine
  (optional)
2 tablespoons butter

100g (3½oz) Parmesan,
  grated
200g (7oz) sprouting
  broccoli, halved
200g (7oz) ceps or any
  other mushroom that
  takes your fancy
1 garlic clove, crushed
1 spring onion, sliced

Heat the stock or water in a pan and keep at a gentle simmer. When making this dish it is very important to keep the stock simmering at all times, otherwise you may interrupt the cooking process.

Heat 1 tablespoon of the oil in a large saucepan over a medium heat. Add the diced onion and cook for 2–3 minutes until softened and just beginning to colour. Gradually add the spelt to the pan and stir well for 1 minute. Once the grains have absorbed all the moisture in the saucepan, deglaze the pan with the white wine and reduce the heat. Again, you must stir gently until all the alcohol has evaporated before adding more liquid.

Add 1 ladle of hot stock to the spelt and stir gently. Let the spelt absorb the stock before adding the next ladle. This slow method keeps the grain firm and concentrates the flavour of the dish. Repeat this process until the spelt

is *al dente* – cooked, yet still with a little bite. This should take about 40–45 minutes. When you feel the spelt has got the right texture briskly stir in the butter and Parmesan. You should have a perfectly glossy finish.

Blanch the sprouting broccoli in a pan of boiling salted water for 2 minutes. Drain and set aside.

If necessary, cut the mushrooms to a similar size. In a large frying pan, heat the remaining olive oil over a medium–high heat. Add the mushrooms together with the garlic and toss them around so that they cook evenly for 2 minutes, or until the mushrooms have lightly browned. Add the sprouting broccoli and season to taste with salt and pepper.

Serve the 'risotto' topped with the broccoli and mushroom mixture, then sprinkle the spring onions all over the plate and devour.

# Whole Grilled Squid with Red Rice and Fresh Herbs

*Squid is a great sustainable fish option that is easy to cook in seconds. This recipe is amazing if you have an outside barbecue and it's the kind of dish that the whole Roux clan loves eating when in the south of France. Obviously, a griddle pan will also do the trick and taste just as fantastic!*

**serves 4**

4 small-medium whole
  squid, cleaned
300g (10½oz) red rice
750ml (1¼ pints) water
3 tablespoons olive oil,
  for drizzling
20g (³⁄₄oz) mixed fresh
  herbs, such as tarragon,
  dill, coriander and
  parsley
salt and freshly ground
  black pepper

**For the marinade:**

2 red chillies, deseeded
  and roughly chopped
½ stick of lemongrass,
  roughly chopped
grated zest and juice of
  1 lemon, plus extra
  grated zest to garnish
1 tablespoon soy sauce
4 tablespoons olive oil
1 garlic clove, crushed
1 handful of mint leaves,
  finely sliced

To make the marinade, place the chillies and lemongrass in a large bowl together with the lemon juice and zest, soy sauce, olive oil and crushed garlic.

Wipe the squid with a dry cloth or kitchen paper to remove any remaining impurities, then place them in the bowl and rub the marinade all over. Sprinkle the mint leaves over the top of the squid with a couple of pinches of pepper. Cover with clingfilm and leave in the fridge for at least 1 hour.

Meanwhile, rinse the red rice under cold water before putting it in a medium saucepan filled with the measured water and a pinch of salt. Once boiling, reduce the heat and leave the rice to simmer covered with a lid for 40–45 minutes. Once cooked, drain the rice, place it in a bowl and drizzle the olive oil over the top.

Remove the squid from the marinade without discarding any excess oil or garnish. This will season the pan and avoid the seafood sticking to it. Heat a griddle pan to as hot as possible to get those special charred marks on the squid without overcooking them. Cook for 2 minutes on each side, until beautifully tender.

Rinse your freshly plucked herbs under cold water and gently dry them off on a piece of paper. These little leaves add freshness and an extra crunch to the dish. Serve the squid on a bed of red rice with the herbs and extra grated lime zest over the top.

# Lobster Ravioli with a Parsley Condiment and Bisque Sauce

*Emily: I absolutely love lobster. It is such a special ingredient, but is only eaten on rare occasions and celebrations. I always savour every single bite.*

**serves 6 as a starter and 4 as a main course**

1kg (2lb 4oz) lobster or
  2 × 600g (1lb 5oz)
  lobsters
2 tablespoons olive oil
1 shallot, finely chopped
¼ bunch of flat-leaf
  parsley, finely chopped
1 drop of Tabasco sauce
sea salt and freshly
  ground black pepper
1 handful of microherbs,
  to garnish (optional)

**For the pasta dough:**
300g (10½oz) '00' flour,
  plus extra for dusting
a generous pinch of salt
150g (5½oz) egg yolk
  (or 7 yolks)
1 tablespoon water
  (optional)

**For the bisque:**
1 tablespoon olive oil
2 tablespoons butter
1 celery stick, roughly
  chopped
½ shallot, roughly chopped

1 garlic clove, crushed
2 tomatoes, chopped
2 tablespoons cognac
500ml (18fl oz) fish stock
  or water

**For the condiment:**
1 bunch of flat-leaf
  parsley
1 salted anchovy
1 teaspoon white wine
  vinegar
2 tablespoons olive oil

First, make the pasta dough. Place the flour, salt and egg yolks in a large bowl and mix together by hand until it is an elastic dough. You may need to add 1 tablespoon water to help knead the dough properly. Wrap the dough in clingfilm and leave to rest in the fridge overnight.

The next day, prepare the lobster. Fill a large casserole dish with water and sea salt. Bring the water to a rolling boil. Kill the lobster instantly by putting a knife straight through its head. Leave the rubber bands on the pincers of the lobster until just before you submerge them in the pot. Place the lobster into the water head first, cover with a lid and cook for 8 minutes for a 1kg (2lb 4oz) lobster or 6 minutes for 2 × 600g (1lb 5oz) lobsters, until the lobster is bright red and has firmed up. Remove from the heat and leave to cool in a bowl of ice-cold water, then remove the shell in 3 sections: the tail, the knuckles and the claws. Leave the tail to one side with a wet cloth on top to keep in the moisture. Keep all the carcasses to make the bisque. Shred the claw and knuckle meat for the ravioli filling and set aside.

Heat 1 tablespoon of the oil in a pan, add the shallot and cook until tender. Remove from the heat and leave to cool, then place it in a mixing bowl with the shredded claw meat and the finely chopped parsley. Season to taste with salt, pepper and the Tabasco and combine with the remaining oil. Using the palms of your hands, roll out the mixture into small balls, about 2cm (¾ inch) wide. Leave in the fridge until the pasta dough is rolled out.

Continues over the page...

# Lobster Ravioli continued

Roll out the chilled pasta dough as finely as you possibly can on a lightly floured surface. It is much easier to use a pasta roller if you have one. The dough will fight you and bounce back but continue until it is 2mm (1/16 inch) thick. Once you have a long strip of pasta dough, place the balls of filling spaced every 6–8 cm (2½–3¼ inches) apart. Cut out squares around the fillings and brush the pasta dough with a little water before folding over diagonally. Tightly seal opposite corners of each pasta square with your fingers, then, with the point of the triangle facing you, bring the other 2 edges together and press them together to form the ravioli shape.

For the bisque, smash the lobster carcasses with the back of a pan until they are small pieces. Heat the oil in a large saucepan over a medium heat and sear the lobster pieces for 4 minutes. Add the butter and roast the carcasses until the butter is foamy. Add the celery, shallot and garlic. When the vegetables are tender, incorporate the diced tomatoes. Deglaze the pan with the cognac and add the fish stock. Simmer for 25 minutes. Strain the bisque, making sure to get the maximum amount of juices from the lobster carcasses. You may need to reduce the bisque for a further 5 minutes to get the right consistency.

For the condiment, place the parsley, anchovy, vinegar and oil in a small blender and season to taste, then blitz well until it is a paste.

Cook the ravioli in boiling salted water for 3 minutes then drain. Slice the lobster tail into 2cm (¾ inch) pieces and, if required, reheat it in the bisque (do not overcook). Place 3 or 4 ravioli on each plate with pieces of lobster tail and 1 tablespoon each of condiment and bisque. Garnish with microherbs, if liked, then serve.

International
Influences

# Emily

I've always enjoyed different kinds of food –
Japanese, Italian, Chinese, South-east Asian
– but Chinese is probably my very favourite.
French food, of course, is known all around the
world and that is usually what the French stick
to. It seems to me that so many Japanese chefs
in Paris cook French food – why not Japanese?
England is so different. Here we embrace other
cuisines and do them well. Paris is trying but
London is way ahead.

All three of us love travelling and trying
different cuisines. And it's so easy now to cook
them at home. We can buy almost any ingredient
we want in the UK – online if not in stores –
so why shut yourself off from that? But at the
same time we don't want to lose sight of our
French roots.

I've learned so much from travelling and working
in different countries and I have picked up lots
of techniques and manners of cooking that I like
to use in my own way. My repertoire ranges from
Italian dishes, such as gnocchi and risotto
to Thai curries and Vietnamese spring rolls.
I learned to love seaweed when working in Japan
and have made a Japanese-inspired seaweed salad
with crayfish tails (*see* page 169).

# Risotto alla Milanese

*This saffron-infused risotto is the pride of Milan.*

**serves 6 as a 'primi'**
**or starter**

250g (9oz) bone marrow
  (this includes the weight
  of the bone)
2 litres (3½ pints)
  chicken stock
2 tablespoons olive oil
1 white onion, finely
  chopped (into pieces the
  size of a grain of rice)

250g (9oz) carnaroli rice
100ml (3½fl oz) white wine
1 pinch of saffron threads
60g (2¼oz) Parmesan,
  finely grated
35g (1¼oz) cold butter,
  cubed
salt and freshly ground
  black pepper

Preheat the oven to 120°C (250°F), Gas Mark ½.

Place the whole bone marrow in a large ovenproof dish and cover with cold water. Add 1 teaspoon salt and bake in the oven for 3 hours. After the time has elapsed, remove the dish from the heat and leave to cool until you can remove the bone from the liquid with your hands. Do not discard the broth (it's delicious); simply add it to the chicken stock. Scoop out the marrow from the bone and cut into small cubes.

Place the chicken stock and cooking broth in a large saucepan and bring to a gentle simmer. Skim the top with a slotted spoon to remove any impurities.

Heat the olive oil in a large saucepan over a medium heat. Add the chopped onion and cook for 3–4 minutes until tender, but not coloured. Add the diced bone marrow followed by the rice and toast the rice for

3 minutes until all the fat has been absorbed by the starch. Season with a pinch of salt and pepper, then deglaze the pan with the white wine and keep stirring with a wooden spatula until all the alcohol has evaporated. At this point, reduce the heat to a gentle simmer and add the first ladleful of stock. Risotto cooks for approximately 17 minutes, so keep feeding the rice with ladles of stock and stirring occasionally. After 15 minutes, add the saffron to the pan. The rice should have doubled in volume and absorbed nearly all of the liquid.

In the last remaining minutes sprinkle the Parmesan and butter into the pan and stir vigorously. Risotto should not be stodgy, so don't be afraid of adding an extra ladle of stock if needed. Check for seasoning before serving.

# Warm Thai Noodle Salad with Seared Beef and Peanuts

*This Thai-inspired noodle salad is the perfect dish to feed a large hungry family.*

**serves 4**

250g (9oz) thick rice
  noodles
1 tablespoon rapeseed oil
250g (9oz) rump steak
4 baby sweetcorns,
  halved
½ carrot, sliced into
  julienne (similar to
  matchsticks)
½ cucumber, sliced into
  julienne

45g soya beans (edamame)
25g (1oz) peanuts, crushed
10 large mint leaves,
  finely sliced
1 tablespoon black sesame
  seeds
1 spring onion, finely
  sliced
1 handful of coriander
  leaves

**For the dressing:**

1cm (½ inch) piece of
  fresh root ginger,
  peeled and grated
½ garlic clove, grated
1 small red chilli,
  deseeded and finely
  sliced
4 tablespoons soy sauce
2 tablespoons sesame oil
2 tablespoons lemon juice
1 tablespoon fish sauce

Soak the noodles in a large bowl of boiling water until soft, then drain and leave to cool with the rapeseed oil added to the noodles to prevent them sticking together.

To prepare the dressing, simply whisk all the ingredients together in a small bowl until everything is well combined. Set aside.

Heat a griddle pan over a medium–high heat. Brush the beef with a little of the dressing and sear for 2½ minutes on each side, depending on the thickness, for a pink centre. Remove from the pan and leave to rest and cool. Repeat with the baby sweetcorns, cooking them for 4–5 minutes until they are a beautiful charred colour. Set aside.

Once the noodles are lukewarm place them in a large bowl. Mix in the sliced vegetables, soy beans and baby sweetcorn, then pour the dressing over the top and combine together with the peanuts and mint leaves. Finely slice the meat while still warm and arrange on top of the salad.

Serve with a sprinkle of sesame seeds, spring onion and coriander leaves.

# *Vitello Tonnato*

*This is another Italian favourite. This cold starter always gets everybody's thumbs up!*

**serves 4**

500g (1lb 2oz) loin of veal
1 egg yolk
1 tablespoon Dijon mustard
1 tablespoon white wine
  vinegar
200ml (7fl oz) neutral oil,
  such as rapeseed or
  sunflower

5 anchovy fillets
1 tablespoon capers
150g (5½oz) canned tuna
  in olive oil
salt and freshly ground
  black pepper
150g (5½oz) lamb's
  lettuce, to serve

Season the meat with salt and pepper before wrapping it tightly in clingfilm. Carefully put the meat into a pan of simmering water for approximately 20 minutes, depending on how you like to eat your meat. Once it is cooked, remove the meat from the pan and leave to rest for 1 hour before putting it in the fridge overnight. It will be a lot easier to slice when cold.

To make the sauce mix the egg yolk, mustard and vinegar together in a bowl. While whisking, gradually pour in the oil until the sauce emulsifies. Put all the remaining ingredients in another bowl and, using a hand-held blender, mix together until it is a smooth paste. You may need to add 2 tablespoons of water to get the right consistency. Combine both sauces together and season with salt and pepper.

Usually the veal is sliced very finely, but in this case, cut into rectangles for more texture. Serve with a lot of sauce and well-seasoned lamb's lettuce.

# Vietnamese Spring Rolls with Spicy Dipping Sauce

*These super-healthy fresh spring rolls summarize just about everything there is to love about Vietnamese food. Once you've mastered the basics, you can play around with this recipe to your heart's content.*

**serves 4**

60g (2¼oz) vermicelli
  rice noodles
1 tablespoon sesame oil
8 × 20cm (8 inch) round
  rice paper wrappers
100g (3½oz) cooked pork
  fillet, finely sliced into
  4 × 5cm (2 inch) strips
1 carrot, cut into
  julienne (similar to
  matchsticks)

1 cucumber, cut into
  julienne
1 spring onion, cut into
  julienne
50g (1¾oz) soya
  beansprouts
4 tablespoons sweet chilli
  sauce
1 handful of mint leaves
1 handful of coriander
  leaves

**For the spicy dipping
sauce:**
1 small red chilli,
  deseeded and finely
  chopped
1 teaspoon grated ginger
1 teaspoon grated garlic
3 tablespoons fish sauce
1 tablespoon soy sauce
juice of ½ lemon
1 tablespoon finely chopped
  coriander stalks

First, make the dipping sauce. Whisk all the ingredients together in a small bowl and leave to infuse for 2 hours. If you are not too keen on 'bits', then pass the sauce through a sieve into a small bowl.

Soak the vermicelli in a heatproof bowl of cold water for 20 minutes, then drain and return the noodles to the bowl. Bring a large saucepan of water to a rolling boil and pour over the noodles until they are completely submerged. After 3 minutes they should all become detached and limp. Once tender, drain and lightly rinse under cold water. Once the noodles are at room temperature, place them back into a bowl and mix in the sesame oil to prevent them sticking. Set aside covered with a damp cloth.

Dip the rice paper wrappers, one at a time, in a bowl of warm water, long enough to soften them. Gently remove from the water and lay flat on the work surface or ideally a plastic chopping board. Arrange all the ingredients, except the mint and coriander leaves, with a dollop of chilli sauce together in a line at the top one-third of the paper so there is plenty of surface area left to roll. Begin to roll, carefully and tightly, tucking in the edges as you go along. When halfway, alternately place the mint and coriander leaves in a line through the middle. These will appear on top of the rolls as a tasty and beautiful decoration.

As you can imagine, eating these fresh as you roll them is best, dipped into the spicy dipping sauce.

# Asian-style Stone Bass

*Marinating fish is not only super healthy; it's also a great way to pack extra flavour in to the delicate flesh. For those who think raw fish can be a little bland, try this recipe out!*

**serves 4**

2 stone bass fillets, about
  500g (1lb 2oz) each
½ garlic clove, very
  finely chopped
1 small red chilli,
  deseeded, if desired,
  and very finely chopped
  (optional)
1 teaspoon Dijon mustard
1 teaspoon honey

1 tablespoon olive oil
1 teaspoon sesame oil
1 tablespoon soy sauce
1 spring onion, chopped
½ bunch of salad cress
finely grated zest of
  1 lime

**For the marinade:**
15g (½oz) juniper berries
15g (½oz) freshly ground
  black pepper

250g (9oz) fine salt
250g (9oz) sea salt
200g (7oz) caster sugar

**To serve (optional):**
caviar or lump fish eggs
mixed salad leaves
fresh mixed herbs

First, make the marinade. Blitz the juniper berries, pepper and salts in a blender, then cover the fish in the salt mixture and sugar and leave to marinate in the fridge for 12 hours. This will season and harden the flesh making it easier to slice.

After 12 hours, rinse the fish and dry with kitchen paper before using.

Place the garlic and the red chilli in a small bowl with the mustard and honey. Drizzle in the oils and the soy sauce and mix together to make an Asian dressing.

Slice the fish into very thin slices and spread it out on a plate, then sprinkle with spring onion, salad cress and lime zest. Season with the Asian dressing.

For a bit of added glamour you can serve this with a little caviar or lump fish eggs, if liked. Mixed salad leaves and fresh mixed herbs are also good additions.

# Green Chicken Curry

*Bursting with flavour, there's nothing quite like a homemade curry.*
*Quick and easy to prepare, this recipe will be thoroughly enjoyed*
*by all the family — bold flavours and hugely satisfying.*

**serves 4**

2 lemongrass sticks
1cm (½ inch) piece of
   fresh root ginger,
   peeled
600ml (20fl oz) coconut
   milk
125ml (4fl oz) chicken
   stock or water
2 bunches of coriander
   (reserve a few leaves
   for the garnish)

500g (1lb 2oz) chicken
   thighs, cut into bite-
   sized pieces
2 tablespoons coconut oil
1 white onion, chopped
1 carrot, chopped
1 green chilli or small
   green pepper, halved
   and deseeded
1 teaspoon shop-bought
   green curry paste
1 kaffir lime leaf
juice of 1 lemon

1 spring onion, finely
   chopped
salt and freshly ground
   black pepper
cooked basmati rice,
   to serve

Blitz the lemongrass, ginger, coconut milk, stock and coriander thoroughly in a powerful blender until the coriander leaves and lemongrass have completely disappeared. Press the liquid mixture through a sieve, making sure you extract as much liquid as you possibly can. Set aside.

Season the chicken. Heat the coconut oil in a large saucepan over a high heat. Sear the chicken until beautifully caramelized. Remove from the pan and set aside. (The chicken is purposefully not cooked through as it will continue cooking in the curry later on.)

Add the onion, carrot and green chilli to the same pan that the chicken was seared in and mix in the curry paste. Once the vegetables are tender, return the chicken to the pan, then pour over the reserved liquid mixture, add the kaffir lime leaf and bring to the boil. Reduce the heat and simmer for 30 minutes. Season to taste, then add the lemon juice and the spring onion. This is best served with basmati rice and the reserved fresh coriander leaves on top.

# Japanese Seaweed Salad with Crayfish Tails

*In Japan they eat seaweed for breakfast lunch and dinner. Sea vegetables have a delicious taste, they are also extremely easy to prepare and are one of the richest sources of minerals around, as well as being virtually fat-free. Wakame and hijiki are sea vegetables and can be bought from Asian food stores or purchased online.*

**serves 4 as a side**

20g (¾oz) dehydrated shredded wakame
10g (¼oz) dehydrated hijiki
1 tablespoon rice vinegar
2 tablespoons sesame oil
1 tablespoon soy sauce

1 teaspoon yuzu or lime juice
1 teaspoon runny honey
1 teaspoon finely grated ginger
120g (4¼oz) cooked crayfish tails

½ nori sheet
1 spring onion, finely sliced
2 tablespoons toasted white sesame seeds

Place the wakame and hijiki seaweed in a large bowl and pour over enough warm water to cover completely. Soak for 10–20 minutes depending on how firm you like the salad to be.

Meanwhile, in a separate bowl, whisk all the liquids together with the honey and grated ginger to make a Japanese dressing. Once the seaweed is soaked, drain and press between your hands to remove any excess water.

Place the seaweed and crayfish tails in a serving bowl and pour the Japanese dressing on top. Toss all the ingredients together until well combined.

Finely slice the nori sheet into fine spaghetti-like strings using a sharp knife or scissors. Just before serving, sprinkle the finely sliced spring onion, sesame seeds and nori all over the salad.

# *Ravioles*

*Emily: I discovered these amazing gnocchi-like pasta a few years back in a small town in the Occitan Valley in Piedmont. Their unusual name comes from a local dialect of Occitan, but these are nothing like traditional Italian ravioli. My husband's 'Nonna' would hand-roll them on a wooden surface and serve them with browned butter and Parmesan. This recipe was passed to me by my mother-in-law.*

**serves 4**

700g (1lb 9oz) potatoes
150–200g (5½–7oz) plain
  flour, plus extra for
  dusting
75g (2¾oz) butter
100g (3½oz) Parmesan,
  grated
salt

Cook the potatoes whole in a pan of boiling water until tender. Once cooked, peel and pass through a potato ricer. The potato pulp must still be piping hot when you transfer it to a lightly floured surface. Gradually knead in the flour as you would for a bread dough. You must have the right consistency to be able to roll out the *ravioles* correctly – not too soft and not too firm.

Roll out the entire potato mix into long sausages of approximately 2cm (¾ inch) wide. Cut the sausages into small pieces, about 2cm (¾ inch) long with a knife. Roll each piece against the floured surface with the palm of your hand to give a long, thin shape.

Once all the *ravioles* have been rolled out, cook them immediately in a pan of boiling salted water for 2 minutes. Drain carefully, as they are very fragile, and place in a warm bowl.

Meanwhile, put the butter in a small saucepan over a medium–low heat and whisk constantly until little browned bits appear on the base. Remove the pan from the heat and pour 2 tablespoons of browned butter over the fresh pasta with some grated Parmesan.

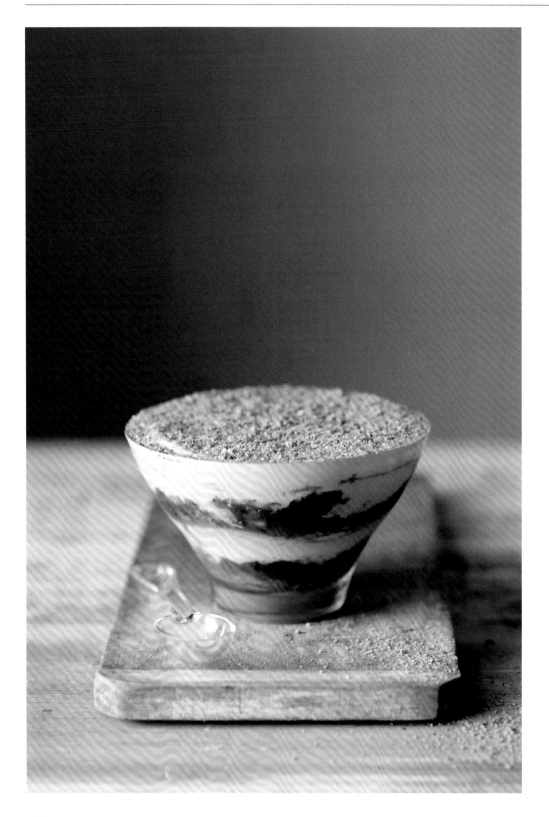

# Strawberry Tiramisu

*All there is to say is YUM! Joconde biscuit is a light almond sponge cake, named after the Mona Lisa. It is traditionally used in the classic French Opera Cake.*

**serves 6–8 and fills a 22cm (8½ inch) round dessert dish or 6–8 small dessert dishes**

230g (8oz) fresh
  strawberries, hulled and
  cut into small cubes,
  about 5mm (¼ inch)
175g (6oz) strawberry jam,
  preferably homemade
1 tablespoon water
  (optional)

**For the strawberry syrup:**
90g (3oz) caster sugar
90ml (3fl oz) water
70g (2½oz) ripe
  strawberries, chopped

**For the Joconde biscuit:**
5 whole eggs
125g (4½oz) ground almonds
125g (4½oz) icing sugar
30g (1oz) plain flour
30g (1oz) clarified butter,
  melted and still hot
4 egg whites
1 pinch of salt

**For the mascarpone cream:**
6 egg yolks
75g (2¾oz) caster sugar
250g (9oz) mascarpone
100ml (3½fl oz) whipping
  cream
1 tablespoon icing sugar

**For the caramelized pistachio powder:**
4 tablespoons caster sugar
2 tablespoons water
75g (2¾oz) toasted
  pistachio nuts

To prepare the strawberry syrup, which can be made well in advance, bring the sugar, measured water and strawberries to the boil, then reduce the heat and simmer for 4 minutes before removing the pan from the heat. Leave the liquid to cool before passing through a sieve. Set aside.

To prepare the Joconde biscuit, preheat the oven to 180°C (350°F), Gas Mark 4 and line 2 or 3 baking trays with greaseproof paper. Place the whole eggs, ground almonds and icing sugar in a large bowl. Whisk with a hand-held mixer until foamy and doubled in volume, then gently sift in the flour and add the clarified butter, gently folding everything together with a spatula.

In a separate bowl, whisk the egg whites with a pinch of salt until nice and stiff, then gently stir one-third of the beaten whites to the egg mixture. Finally, pour the entire egg mixture on top of the remaining egg white and combine gently, making sure not to break the egg whites.

Pour the mixture onto 2 or 3 baking trays. Evenly spread out with a spatula until it is 1–1.5 cm (½–⅝ inch) thick and bake in the oven for 10–15 minutes until lightly golden but still moist and soft. When cooked, flip the biscuit onto a work surface and gently remove the greaseproof paper. Leave to cool before cutting into the shape of your tin.

Continues over the page...

# Strawberry Tiramisu continued

To make the mascarpone cream, make sure that both creams and yolks are cold before you start. Whisk the egg yolks and caster sugar together in a bowl with a hand-held mixer until white and foamy. Gradually add the mascarpone and beat on a medium speed for at least 8 minutes until the mixture has doubled in volume and has a ribbon texture.

In a separate bowl, whip the cream and icing sugar together until stiff peaks form and it is smooth and unctuous. Gently fold both mixtures together and store in the fridge until ready to build the tiramisu.

For the caramelized pistachio powder, line a baking tray with greaseproof paper. Pour the sugar and measured water into a small saucepan over a medium–low heat. Once the sugar has dissolved, increase the heat and boil. There's no need to stir until the syrup begins to colour. At this point add the pistachios and stir with a wooden spoon until it is a beautiful caramel colour. Once all the nuts are properly coated, spread them on the prepared baking tray and leave to cool until the caramel has hardened. Once the caramel has hardened, break the bits off and pulse in a powerful blender until ground to a powder.

Mix the strawberries and jam together. If you have quite a liquid jam simply mix both together. If the jam is a little stiff, lightly heat and add the measured water before mixing with the fresh strawberries.

Begin layering a 22cm (8½ inch) round dessert dish or 6–8 individual dessert dishes. Soak the Joconde biscuit in the strawberry syrup and place a layer on the base of the dish(es), then evenly spread the jam and strawberry mixture over, followed by the mascarpone cream. Repeat the process until you reach the top of the dish(es) making sure you finish off by sprinkling with the caramelized pistachio powder.

# Lychee and Coconut Panna Cotta Infused with Kaffir Lime Leaves

*The aromas in this dessert are reminiscent of Asia. Kaffir limes and their leaves deliver unmistakable aromatic flavours and, paired with the delicate sweetness of lychee and coconut, this panna cotta is like no other.*

serves 4–6

For the panna cotta:
400g (14oz) can pitted
  lychees in their liquid
400ml (14fl oz) can coconut
  milk
1 tablespoon caster sugar
2 kaffir lime leaves
5 × 2g (¹⁄₁₆oz) sheets of
  gelatine
250ml (9fl oz) double cream

For the crispy coconut flakes:
150g (5½oz) coconut flakes
1 pinch of salt
1 tablespoon maple syrup

Preheat the oven to 180°C (350°F), Gas Mark 4.

To prepare the crispy coconut flakes, mix the coconut, salt and maple syrup in a large bowl and stir until the coconut is evenly coated all over. Spread the mixture on a baking sheet and bake in the oven for 20 minutes, stirring every 5–7 minutes, until the coconut flakes are an even golden brown colour. Remove from the oven and leave to cool.

For the panna cotta, blitz the lychees and their liquid in a powerful food processor until paste-like, then pass through a fine-mesh sieve to form a smooth paste. Place this paste together with the coconut milk, sugar and kaffir lime leaves in a saucepan and bring to a gentle simmer, then remove from the heat. Cover with a lid and leave to infuse for approximately 15 minutes. Remove the kaffir leaves with a slotted spoon and discard.

Soak the gelatine sheets in a bowl of cold water for 2–3 minutes until softened, then squeeze out the excess water and whisk into the warm liquid. Finally, pour in the cream then stir the mixture before using it to fill 4–6 × 200ml (7fl oz) ramekins.

Leave the panna cotta to set in the refrigerator for at least 3 hours. Sprinkle the crispy coconut flakes over the top for that special crunch before devouring.

# The Professional
# Kitchen

# Emily

I went to the great Institut Paul Bocuse
catering college in France so I have quite a
bit of knowledge of traditional French cookery.
But since then I have worked both in traditional
and more modern restaurants, so the recipes in
this chapter are inspired by what I have learned
in both. I love to adapt the old techniques and
let my imagination take over to create something
different. For instance, duck breast is a
stalwart of French menus but I have suggested
partnering it with asparagus and coffee (*see* page
200) and my pan-seared pollock is served with
avocado and a citrus dressing (*see* page 184).
Both dishes are still very French but with a
lighter touch that suits today's tastes - this
is the kind of food that I really enjoy.

Some of these recipes, such as the Crispy
Rolled Pig's Head with Red Cabbage Salad
(*see* page 219), are quite challenging and take
a while to put together, but they are perfectly
achievable for the home cook and so worth the
effort - mum has tried them in our kitchen.
Once in a while it's good to test your skills
and try something a little more adventurous.

# Pan-seared Pollock with Avocado and Citrus Dressing

*Avocado is an incredibly healthy and versatile fruit that can be used in savoury dishes. It is grilled in this recipe and puréed with a sharp and tangy citrus dressing. You are sure to impress your guest with this fun dish.*

**serves 4**

800g (1lb 12oz) pollock
  fillets, scaled
1 tablespoon olive oil
salt and freshly ground
  black pepper
coriander cress, to
  garnish

**For the avocado purée:**
1½ avocados, peeled and
  stoned
juice of ½ lemon
2 drops of Tabasco sauce

2 tablespoons olive oil
¼ bunch of coriander

**For the lemon dressing:**
125ml (4fl oz) lemon juice
1 tablespoon caster sugar
3 lemons, peeled and
  quartered
3 tablespoons olive oil
finely grated zest of
  ½ lemon
1 pinch of chilli powder
½ avocado, peeled and cut
  into 12 small cubes,
  about 5mm (¼ inch)

**For the garnish:**
2 pak choi, halved
2 tablespoons water
1 tablespoon olive oil
1 avocado, peeled, stoned
  and cut into segments

To make the lemon dressing, put the lemon juice and sugar with the quartered peeled lemons (do not remove the pips) into a small saucepan and simmer over a low heat for approximately 40 minutes. Once the lemon chunks have dissolved and the juice has reduced by half, pass through a sieve and set the liquid paste aside to cool. Once the lemon paste has cooled, whisk in a small bowl together with the olive oil. To complete the dressing incorporate the lemon zest, chilli powder and avocado cubes before seasoning to taste. Don't discard the avocado trimmings as you can use them in the avocado purée.

To prepare the avocado purée, put the avocados in a powerful blender together with the lemon juice, Tabasco, olive oil, coriander and a pinch of salt and blend until the purée is silky smooth. You might need to add a little water if the avocados are not ripe enough. Set aside.

Season the fish with salt and pepper before pan-searing skin-side down in the olive oil in a large frying pan over a medium heat. Once the skin is crispy and lightly coloured, roughly 3 minutes, turn the fish over and cook for a further 1 minute depending on the size of the fish. Set aside.

For the garnish, sear the pak choi in the same pan for 2 minutes and deglaze with the measured water. Once the water has completely evaporated, the greens should be tender and cooked through.

Lightly oil a nonstick frying pan with the oil, then pan-sear each avocado segment carefully for 2 minutes on each side. Once the avocado segments are coloured on each side remove from the pan.

Delicately arrange all the ingredients on 4 plates and garnish with coriander cress.

# Spatchcocked Chicken with Morels, Spring Onions and Watercress

*Deboning is a very classic skill, but not that difficult to master. Nearly any bird can be spatchcocked and cooked the same way. It guarantees crispy skin and easy eating and carving.*

**serves 4**

1 whole chicken (about
  1.4kg/3lb 3oz)
4 tablespoons olive oil
80g (3oz) dried morels or
  240g (8½oz) fresh morels

1 shallot, finely chopped
1 tablespoon butter
100ml (3½fl oz) vin jaune
  (a sherry-like wine from
  France's Jura region) or
  dry sherry
200ml (7fl oz) chicken stock

100ml (3½fl oz) double
  cream
8 spring onions, trimmed
100g (3½oz) baby
  watercress
salt and freshly ground
  black pepper

Place the chicken, breast-side down, on a chopping board and cut through the middle from front to rear with a sharp knife. Carefully follow the bones all the way round until you have removed the whole carcass, cutting through the thigh and wing joint. You should be left with a completely deboned chicken, preferably without any holes in it. Season the chicken flesh with a pinch of salt and pepper.

Heat 2 tablespoons of the olive oil in a large nonstick frying pan over a medium–low heat. When the oil is hot, place the chicken, skin-side down, into the pan. Place a round piece of greaseproof paper on top of the chicken and put a heavy pan on top to weigh it down and flatten. Leave to cook for 30–40 minutes checking it occasionally. Remove the weight from the chicken and check that the thighs are cooked through and the skin is golden and crisp. Remove from the heat and leave to rest for at least 10 minutes.

Rehydrate the morels in a bowl of warm water for at least 15 minutes. Drain them and check for any remaining grit, rinsing them under cold water if necessary.

Heat 1 tablespoon of the olive oil in a large frying pan over a medium heat. Add the chopped shallot and morels to the pan. Stir until the shallot are translucent, approximately 3 minutes. Season to taste. Add the butter to the pan and let the mushrooms crisp up for a further 3 minutes. Once the morels have absorbed all the fat, deglaze with the vin jaune. As soon as the alcohol has evaporated pour the stock into the pan. Leave to simmer and reduce by two-thirds for 5–10 minutes, depending on the pan size. Finally, finish the sauce by incorporating the cream and bringing to the boil for 2 minutes. Check the seasoning again before plating up.

Bring a saucepan of salted water to the boil and blanch the spring onions for 30 seconds, then refresh in a bowl of iced water. Heat a griddle pan and brush with the remaining olive oil before grilling the spring onions, cut-side down, for 4–5 minutes, turning them around occasionally. Once tender and a nice charred colour remove them from the heat.

Cut the chicken into 4 pieces and serve with the spring onions and peppery watercress.

# Mushroom Agnolotti

*The colour, texture and flavour of fresh pasta is simply incomparable to dried pasta.*
*It's best to prepare this dish of small, filled pasta squares in spring, when the mushrooms*
*are at their best. Enjoy it as a starter or as a main course with added vegetables.*

**serves 4**

**For the pasta dough:**
500g (1lb 2oz) plain flour,
  plus extra for dusting
1 teaspoon salt
1 teaspoon olive oil, plus
  extra for drizzling
4 whole eggs
3 tablespoons water
  (optional)

**For the filling:**
300g (10½oz) white
  mushrooms or any in-
  season wild mushrooms,
  such as morels or ceps
60g (2¼oz) Parmesan,
  grated
1 handful of walnuts,
  chopped
50g (1¾oz) dried
  breadcrumbs

½ bunch of chives, chopped
2 tablespoons olive oil
1 garlic clove, finely
  chopped
1 spring onion, finely
  chopped
3 tablespoons double cream
salt and freshly ground
  black pepper

To make the pasta dough, place the flour, salt, olive oil and beaten eggs in a large bowl and mix together by hand until it is elastic. You may need to add a few tablespoons of water to help knead the dough properly. Wrap the dough in clingfilm and leave to rest in the fridge overnight.

The next day, make the filling. Chop three-quarters of the mushrooms. Cut the remaining mushrooms into small cubes and set aside in a bowl. Add the grated Parmesan, chopped walnuts, breadcrumbs and chopped chives to the chopped mushrooms and mix together.

Heat the olive oil in a frying pan over a medium heat and fry the garlic and spring onion for 2–3 minutes, until tender. Add the chopped mushroom mixture and season. Once the mushrooms are cooked and have rendered all their water, deglaze the pan with the cream. Transfer the cooked mixture to a blender and blitz until it is a smooth purée, then leave to cool before mixing it in to the

other ingredients, including the mushroom cubes. Set the filling aside for at least 2 hours in the fridge before using.

Roll out the pasta dough as finely as you possibly can on a lightly floured surface. It is much easier to use a pasta machine if you have one. The dough will fight you and bounce back but continue until it is 2mm (¹⁄₁₆ inch) thick. Cut out squares, about 8cm (3¼ inches) with a sharp knife, then add ½ tablespoon of filling into the centre of each square. Brush a little water around the edge of the pasta squares and fold over diagonally. You should get crossed-top agnolotti.

Cook the pasta in a pan of boiling salted water for 4 minutes, then drain and serve, drizzled with some olive oil. You can also add some wild mushrooms or ceps and a meat jus (beef or veal) to accompany the pasta, if you like.

# Razor Clams, Mushrooms and Wild Garlic

*Emily: Many of my summer holidays were spent trying to trick and catch as many clams as we could for supper. Wild garlic, also known as ramsons, can be found in deciduous woodlands with moist soils. If it's out of season when you prepare this dish, substitute it with coriander cress.*

**serves 1 as a starter**

2 raw extra-large
  razor clams
15g (½oz) St George
  mushrooms
15g (½oz) girolles
1 tablespoon olive oil
1 tablespoon butter

½ spring onion, finely
  sliced
1 tablespoon finely sliced
  wild garlic (optional)
1 pinch of *piment
  d'Espelette* or chilli
  powder
1 pinch of grated lemon
  zest

1 tablespoon toasted
  breadcrumbs
salt and freshly ground
  black pepper
wild garlic flowers
  or coriander cress,
  to garnish

Remove the flesh of the clams and discard the stomachs keeping only the muscle. Reserve in a bowl of ice-cold water until ready to use. Clean the clam shells and set aside.

Make sure that all the mushrooms are the same size and dry before cooking them.

Heat the olive oil in a large frying pan over a medium–high heat. When hot, add the mushrooms, season and sauté for 4–8 minutes, or until they have rendered all their water. Add the butter, spring onion (only the white part) and the wild garlic, if available.

Meanwhile, diagonally slice the razor clams to make 2cm (¾ inch) wide lozenges. Add them to the pan and mix in with all the other ingredients. The shellfish will cook extremely quickly, so remove the pan from the heat after 30 seconds. Sprinkle over the *piment d'Espelette* and lemon zest before starting to plate.

Spoon the cooked mixture into both sides of the cleaned razor clam shells and top with toasted breadcrumbs, wild garlic flowers or coriander cress, and the green parts of sliced spring onion.

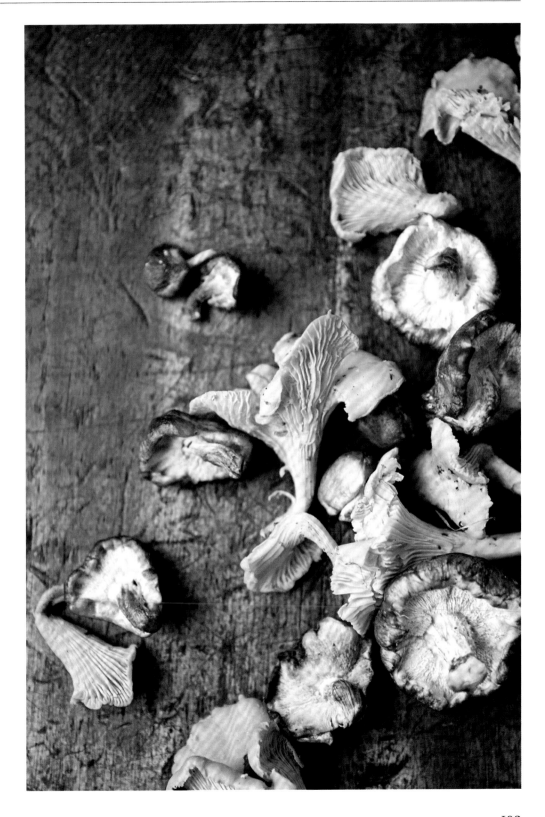

# Octopus Salad with Chilli Mayonnaise

*Octopus is a great alternative to fish. People tend to shy away when it comes to cooking 'the beast', although it is extremely easy. Cooked properly not only is octopus nutritious; it is also amazing in taste and texture.*

serves 4

For the octopus:
1 whole octopus (approx.
  2kg/4lb 8oz) – it will
  reduce considerably in
  size once cooked
1 carrot, roughly chopped
1 white onion, roughly
  chopped
1 bay leaf
4 black peppercorns
1 tablespoon rock salt
butter, for pan-frying

For the mayonnaise:
1 egg yolk
1 teaspoon Dijon mustard
  juice of ½ lemon
250ml (9fl oz) neutral oil,
  such as rapeseed or
  sunflower
1 pinch each of salt and
  freshly ground black
  pepper
1 tablespoon sweet chilli
  sauce

For the salad:
250g (9oz) new potatoes,
  halved
4 tablespoons olive oil
125ml (4fl oz) water
1 pinch each of salt and
  freshly ground black
  pepper
3 large spring onions,
  2 cut in half and
  1 thinly sliced
2 green chillies or baby
  green peppers, deseeded
3 little gem lettuces,
  quartered
1 tablespoon butter,
  plus 1 teaspoon

To prepare the octopus, cut off and discard the head, including the beak, then remove and discard any innards. Place the carrot, onion, bay leaf, peppercorns and rock salt in a large casserole dish, add approximately 2 litres (3½ pints) water and bring to the boil. Add the octopus and check that the water covers it – add more if it doesn't. Reduce the heat and cook the octopus in simmering water for up to 1½ hours – depending on the size of the octopus – until tender (check frequently with a knife). Once you can easily cut through the flesh, drain the octopus and leave to cool before transferring to the fridge overnight.

The next day, make the mayonnaise. Place the egg yolk in a large bowl. Add the mustard and lemon juice and whisk in the oil, drop by drop, until it is well combined. After a few minutes the sauce will emulsify and thicken. Season to taste with salt and pepper and add the sweet chilli sauce.

To make the salad, place the new potatoes in a pan large enough to fit them all in. Add 2 tablespoons of the olive oil and set over a medium heat. Spread out the potatoes flesh-side down and let them colour for 5 minutes. Once they have a nice caramelized brown colour pour in the measured water and cover the pan with a lid. The steam will cook the potatoes. Once the water has completely evaporated, approximately 8 minutes, season with the salt and pepper and set aside.

Continues over the page...

# Octopus Salad continued

Heat a little olive oil in a frying pan over a
medium heat and pan-sear the halved spring
onions for 2–3 minutes, or until tender,
then add the green chillies and pan-sear for
1 minute. Once both the spring onions and
chillies are tender, remove from the heat
and set aside with the potatoes.

Pan-sear the lettuces for a few minutes on
each side in 1 teaspoon of butter. The lettuces
should not be cooked, just charred to give
them extra taste.

Finally, peel any excess skin off the octopus
and slice before pan-frying in 1 tablespoon
of butter for 2 minutes on each side. Once
the octopus is a beautiful brown, caramelized
colour, remove from the pan.

Divide the warm ingredients between
serving plates, add a couple of spoonfuls of
mayonnaise to each plate, and then sprinkle
the finely sliced spring onion on top.

# Smoked Eel with Tea Consommé

*The combination of delicately smoked tea and smoked*
*eel takes this dish to a new dimension.*

**serves 2**

1 red beetroot, any leaves
  cut off
1 yellow beetroot, any
  leaves cut off
olive oil, for drizzling

4 turnips, trimmed but
  keep the tops for use
  in the Radish Top Soup
  (*see* page 28)
200g (7oz) smoked eel
½ tablespoon butter
550ml (19fl oz) clear fish
  stock

1 tablespoon lapsang
  souchong tea
1 spring onion, finely
  sliced
salt and freshly ground
  black pepper

Preheat the oven to 200°C (400°F), Gas Mark 6.

Place the beetroot on some foil, drizzle with olive oil and season with salt and pepper. Wrap the foil around the beetroot loosely and place the package on a baking tray. Roast in the oven for 1½ hours (add 30 minutes for larger veggies) until the tip of a knife easily slides through the middle of the beetroot. Leave the beetroot to cool until you can handle them, then peel off the skin with kitchen paper.

Leave baby turnips whole or cut larger turnips into bite-sized pieces. Wrap them loosely in foil with the same seasoning as the beetroot. Roast the turnips in the oven until tender. Start checking on them after about 30 minutes.

Meanwhile, slice the smoked eel into bite-sized diamond shapes. Heat a drop of olive oil in a nonstick frying pan over a medium–high heat and pan-sear the eel pieces. After 2 minutes, once the eel has a little colour, reduce the heat and add the butter to the pan. Fry for a further 2 minutes with the foaming butter, then remove from the pan and set aside on kitchen paper.

Bring the fish stock to the boil in a medium saucepan. Turn off the heat as soon as the liquid has boiled and sprinkle in the tea. Leave the tea to infuse for approximately 5 minutes (more or less depending on how strong you enjoy it), then pass through a fine sieve and season with salt and pepper.

Slice all the cooked vegetables into small segments and place in two small serving bowls, then delicately add the eel and sprinkle the spring onion on top. Finally, pour over the fish stock.

# Duck Breast, Asparagus and Coffee

*Duck breast, asparagus and coffee make a fantastic combination in this extraordinary dish. They are served drizzled with a subtle orange-flavoured, sweet-and-sour sauce based on a classic French gastrique, which is made from caramelized sugar deglazed with vinegar.*

**serves 4**

2 large duck breasts,
  with skin
12 green asparagus spears
1 tablespoon olive oil
1 handful of chives,
  finely sliced
salt and freshly ground
  black pepper
1 handful of microherbs,
  to garnish (optional)

**For the asparagus purée:**
1 tablespoon olive oil
350g (12oz) white
  asparagus, peeled and
  roughly chopped
2 tablespoons butter
50g (1¾oz) double cream
1 pinch of finely ground
  coffee

**For the pickled onion:**
1 small red onion, sliced
  into thin rings, about
  1–2mm (¹⁄₁₆ inch) thick
20g (¾oz) caster sugar
1 teaspoon salt
½ teaspoon crushed black
  pepper
150ml (¼ pint) white wine
  vinegar
100ml (3½fl oz) water
1 dried bay leaf

**For the gastrique sauce:**
60g (2¼oz) caster sugar
4 tablespoons red wine
  vinegar
juice of 2 oranges
200ml (7fl oz) chicken or
  vegetable stock

The pickled onion can be prepared well in advance. Place the onion rings in a sterilized preserving jar or bowl. Bring all the other ingredients to the boil in a small saucepan. As soon as it has reached a rolling boil, pour the mixture over the sliced onions. Leave the onion rings to cool before sealing the jar or eating.

To make the asparagus purée, heat the olive oil in a large saucepan over a medium heat and add the chopped white asparagus. Stir until the asparagus begin to colour, then add the butter to the pan. Leave the butter to foam up for at least 3 minutes before seasoning and covering with a lid. After 5 minutes uncover and check that all the chunks are tender, then deglaze with the cream and bring to a gentle simmer before pouring everything into a food processor. Blitz for 2 minutes until smooth, then pass through a sieve to get rid of any remaining strings. Season the purée to taste with salt, pepper and the ground coffee.

For the gastrique sauce, place the sugar in a dry saucepan and leave to caramelize over a gentle heat. Once the sugar has entirely dissolved, deglaze the pan with the vinegar.

Once the liquid has evaporated pour in the orange juice together with the stock and leave to simmer for 5–10 minutes until reduced and thickened.

Score the skin of the duck to allow the fat to render away easily and season with a pinch of salt and pepper. Place a large nonstick frying pan over a medium heat. Once nice and hot, place the breasts, skin-side down, in the pan and dry-fry for approximately 7 minutes until golden brown and crispy. Remove some of the fat from the pan before turning the duck over to cook for a further 4 minutes, depending on the thickness of the meat. Leave to rest for at least 5 minutes before serving.

Snap off the ends of the green asparagus spears and peel the bottom half. Bring a large pot of salted water to the boil and add the asparagus. Cook for 5–8 minutes until tender, then drain and refresh in a bowl of iced water. Heat the olive oil in a frying pan over a medium heat and add the asparagus and cook for 3–10 minutes, until they are a beautiful brown caramelized colour. Slice the asparagus into 4 uneven segments and sprinkle the chives all over.

To serve, cut each duck breast lengthways in half, then place a half on each plate. Add a large tablespoon of purée in the centre of each plate and place the asparagus spears on top. Drizzle the gastrique sauce around the plate to finish and garnish with pickled onion and microherbs, if liked.

# Rabbit Pâté en Croute

*Don't be put off by the name of this recipe and the complicated techniques it implies. It is easily achievable at home.*

**serves 8 as a starter**

2 tablespoons butter
1 shallot, sliced
125g (4½oz) rabbit or
  chicken liver
1 thyme sprig
4 tablespoons cognac
125g (4½oz) rabbit meat
125g (4½oz) unsmoked
  bacon rashers
2 juniper berries

125g (4½oz) terrine of
  foie gras, cut into
  small dice
1kg (2lb 4oz) spinach
1 garlic clove, crushed

**For the shortcrust pastry:**
120g (4¼oz) plain flour,
  plus extra for dusting
1 pinch of fine salt
25g (1oz) lard, cubed
25g (1oz) butter, cubed
1-2 tablespoons cold water
1 egg yolk mixed with
  1 tablespoon milk to use
  as an egg wash
salt and freshly ground
  black pepper

To make the pastry, sift the flour and salt into a large mixing bowl. Add the lard together with the butter and rub them between your fingertips until the mixture is crumbly and resembles breadcrumbs. Pour in the water and bring the dough together with your hands, but do not overwork it. Cover the dough and leave to rest in the fridge for 30 minutes before using.

Heat half the butter in a frying pan over a medium heat and cook the shallot for 2–3 minutes, until softened. Increase the heat to high, add the livers and cook until brown and caramelized. Season with salt and pepper, add the thyme and deglaze with the cognac. Once the alcohol has evaporated, leave to cool a little, then transfer to the fridge to cool further.

Preheat the oven to 180°C (350°F), Gas Mark 4.

Mince the rabbit meat, the cooled liver and shallot mixture, the bacon and juniper berries in a mincer, then mix together thoroughly before seasoning and adding the foie gras.

Heat the remaining butter in a frying pan and sauté the spinach and garlic for 3–4 minutes until the spinach is completely wilted, then remove from the heat and leave to cool. Press the cooled spinach in the palms of your hands to extract all the water and form into small round balls.

Line the base and side of a round 15cm (6 inch) tin with the pastry. Spread the minced meat over the base, followed by a layer of the spinach balls, then repeat the layering process until you reach the top of the tin. Roll out the remaining pastry into a thin round to the diameter of your tin to create a lid and brush all over with the egg wash. Cook in the oven for 30–40 minutes.

Variation: For a professional finish you can reduce 300ml (½ pint) chicken stock and add to the pâté by making a small hole in the centre of the lid. Pour the stock inside only once the pâté is cooked and has been chilled overnight. Thanks to this you will achieve a beautiful meaty jelly.

# Pan-seared Mackerel with Cucumber Tagliatelle

*Mackerel is one of the cheapest fish on the market and is invariably oozing with taste.*

**serves 4**

6 mackerel fillets, about
  280–300g (10–10½oz) each
1 cucumber, peeled and cut
  in half lengthways
50ml (2fl oz) water
100ml (3½fl oz) white wine
  vinegar
50g (1¾oz) caster sugar
2 tablespoons olive oil

100g (3½oz) Greek yogurt
1 pinch of paprika
2 mint leaves, finely
  chopped
1 spring onion, very
  finely sliced
finely grated zest of
  1 lime
salt and freshly ground
  black pepper

**For the marinade:**
20g (¾oz) salt per 1kg
  (2lb 4oz) mackerel
2g (¹⁄₁₀oz) sugar per 1kg
  (2lb 4oz) mackerel

Place the mackerel in a shallow dish and sprinkle the salt and sugar over the top. Allow to marinate for 45 minutes before cooking as this will help tenderize and begin to cook the flesh. Carefully wash the marinade off and pat dry with kitchen paper before cooking.

With one half of the cucumber make long tagliatelle-like strips with the help of a mandolin or a vegetable peeler, then bring the measured water, vinegar and sugar to the boil in a pan and add the cucumber strips. Remove the pan from the heat and leave to cool. Once cooled, you should have some tangy cucumber 'tagliatelle'. Discard the remaining liquid.

Cut the other half of the cucumber into chunks and sear them in a frying pan with 1 tablespoon of the olive oil until golden brown. In the same heated pan, sear the mackerel with the remaining oil until the skin is nice and crispy. Set the mackerel aside until they are cold before cutting them into bite-sized pieces. Season the yogurt with salt, pepper, paprika and finely chopped mint. Plate everything together and scatter the spring onion and lime zest over the top.

# Crispy Sweetbreads, Asparagus and Almond Purée

*The whole Roux clan love sweetbreads. The tender and moist*
*texture combined with the crispy exterior is simply heavenly.*

**serves 4**

800g (1lb 12oz) raw veal
  sweetbreads
1 bunch of cherry tomatoes
12 thin green asparagus
2 tablespoons olive oil,
  plus a drizzle for
  baking

a handful of plain flour,
  for dusting
salt and freshly ground
  black pepper

**For the almond purée:**
100g (3½oz) blanched
  almonds
200ml (7fl oz) milk

100ml (3½fl oz) double
  cream

**For the jus:**
500ml (18fl oz) veal stock
200ml (7fl oz) tomato juice
30g (1oz) stoned black
  olives, halved

It is best to soak the sweetbreads for several hours in clean cold water to remove any impurities.

Preheat the oven to 180°C (350°F), Gas Mark 4.

Bring a large pot filled with salted water to a gentle simmer before adding the raw sweetbreads. Depending on the size, cook them for 15–20 minutes making sure the water never boils. Delicately remove the offal from the water and immediately refresh in a bowl of ice-cold water. Trim off any sinew or gristle and pat dry with kitchen paper. Set aside.

To create a simple and light jus to accompany the dish, reduce the stock and tomato juice in 2 separate saucepans for 5–10 minutes until they are both reduced by two-thirds. Pour one into the other and whisk them together, then add the halved olives and season to taste. Set aside.

To make the almond purée, place the blanched almonds in a medium saucepan with the milk and cream and bring to a gentle simmer. Cook for 10 minutes, then while still hot, transfer the almonds and liquid directly to a food processor and blitz until completely smooth. Season well.

Place the cherry tomatoes and asparagus spears in a large bowl and carefully season the veggies with a drizzle of olive oil, salt and pepper. Place on a baking tray and cook in the oven for 12–15 minutes, until the asparagus are tender and the tomatoes are shrivelled up.

Meanwhile, season each sweetbread with salt and pepper and lightly dust in flour. Heat the 2 tablespoons of olive oil in a frying pan over a medium–high heat and pan-fry the sweetbreads for approximately 3–5 minutes on each side. Avoid moving them too often in the pan, in order to achieve that beautiful crispy brown colour.

Elegantly dress all the different elements together and devour.

# Confit Pork, Kale and Kabocha Purée

*This is a colourful and healthy recipe that always pleases a crowd. Kale is an extremely popular vegetable, known for its numerous health benefits. It is also full of flavour and simply very pretty.*

**serves 4**

700g (1lb 9oz) pork belly
2 tablespoons olive oil
salt and freshly ground
  black pepper

**For the pumpkin purée:**
1 whole kabocha squash
  (approx. 550g/1lb 4oz)

30ml (1fl oz) olive oil, plus
  1 tablespoon for cooking
1 tablespoon Dijon mustard

**For the garnish:**
100g (3½oz) flower sprouts
  (cross between a sprout
  and a baby cabbage) or
  cavolo nero

100g (3½oz) sprouting
  broccoli
100g (3½oz) purple kale
2 tablespoons olive oil
1 garlic clove, crushed

**For the glaze:**
200ml (7fl oz) pork or
  chicken stock
1 teaspoon butter

Place the pork belly in a vacuum bag with a pinch of salt and pepper. Seal firmly in a vacuum pack machine and cook in a water bath at 87°C (189°F) for 3½ hours.

Remove the meat from the water bath and place the bag in iced water to immediately stop cooking. Leave the pork belly to cool in the fridge for a further 45 minutes in order to harden and make it easier to slice. Portion the pork belly into slices of approximately 4–5cm (1½–2 inches) wide.

Meanwhile, rinse the squash under cold water to get rid of any residual dirt. Cut it in half and remove the seeds with a spoon. If the skin is thin enough, don't bother peeling it as it will give extra taste and texture to the purée. Roughly chop the squash into bite-sized chunks before searing in a shallow saucepan with 1 tablespoon olive oil. After 2 minutes the chunks should be lightly coloured. Cover the saucepan with a lid and reduce the heat (by doing so, the kabocha will render water) and cook for approximately 20 minutes

until tender throughout and all the water has evaporated from the pan. While still hot, transfer the pumpkin to a powerful blender together with the Dijon mustard, then add the 30ml (1fl oz) olive oil, drop by drop, until the purée emulsifies and thickens. Season to taste with salt and pepper and set aside.

To make the glaze, place the stock in a small saucepan over a low heat and leave to simmer and reduce until the stock becomes a darker colour, nearly syrup-like, about 5–10 minutes. Once you have got the right texture, remove from the heat and whisk in the butter. Set aside.

Blanch the flower sprouts and sprouting broccoli together in a pan of heavily salted boiling water for 2 minutes. This will help to keep the beautiful colour of the vegetables and precook them. Drain carefully and place in a bowl of ice-cold water. Repeat the same process with the purple kale. Heat the olive oil in a large pan over a medium–high heat. Add the crushed garlic together with the flower sprouts, broccoli and kale. Move the greens

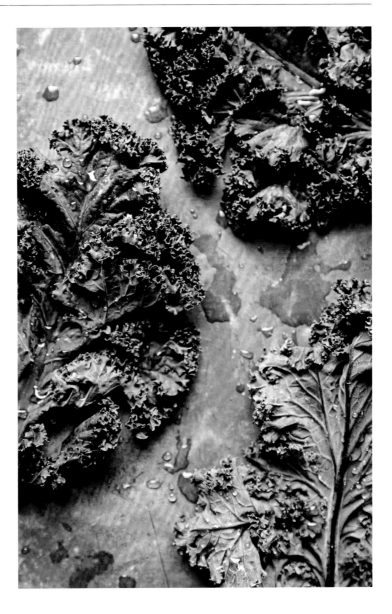

around with tongs, so as not to burn them and sprinkle with salt and pepper. Cook and crisp up for 1 minute.

Pan-sear each portion of pork belly in a large frying pan with a drizzle of olive oil over a medium–high heat. Once all the pieces are a lovely brown caramelized colour reduce the heat and add the reserved sauce to the pan.

Spoon the sauce over each portion of pork to glaze it until it is completely covered in sauce.

Serve immediately with the pumpkin purée and pan-fried vegetables.

# Crispy Rolled Pig's Head with Red Cabbage Salad

*Although this recipe is not for the squeamish, it is absolutely delectable and you can prepare it well in advance. This is a truly wholesome dish that will surprise your guests for sure.*

**serves 4**

1 pig's head

**For the red cabbage salad:**
350g (12oz) red cabbage, finely shredded
2 tablespoons hazelnut oil
2 tablespoons flaked hazelnuts
1 handful of parsley leaves

finely grated zest of ½ lemon
1 teaspoon runny honey
1 tablespoon lemon juice
1 tablespoon olive oil
1 generous pinch of Quatre Épices spice blend, to season
salt and freshly ground black pepper

**For the bouillon:**
1 carrot, roughly chopped
1 white onion, roughly chopped
1 celery stick, roughly chopped
1 star anise
1 bay leaf
1 cinnamon stick
4 black peppercorns

Preheat the oven to 180°C (350°F), Gas Mark 4.

Usually your butcher would have removed all excess hair on the pig's head; however if any is left, use a kitchen blowtorch to remove them. Using a sharp knife, cut all the way down the middle of the head to the snout and follow the bone structure with your knife. Cut the skin and muscle away from the bone until you end up with 2 rectangular pieces of meat with no holes in them.

Season the meat with a pinch of salt, pepper and the spice blend before rolling the pig's head tightly, making sure the ears and snout are folded inside. Tie kitchen string all the way around the rolled head to keep everything in place (as you would with a roast). Place the head in a large casserole dish with the bouillon ingredients and cover with water. Cook in simmering water for about 4 hours. If necessary, top up with water during cooking as the head must always be submerged. Once tender, cooked through and you can easily pierce the meat with a skewer, remove the head, leave to cool, then wrap in clingfilm to keep its shape. Leave in the fridge overnight.

The next day, cover the shredded cabbage with ice-cold water and leave to stand for 15 minutes. Drain. Meanwhile, heat the hazelnut oil in a wok or large frying pan over a high heat. Once the wok is piping hot, sprinkle in the cabbage and toss around for 2 minutes. You must keep the crunch and freshness of the raw vegetable. Remove from the heat, place in a bowl and incorporate the remaining ingredients, except the olive oil.

At the last minute, cut the pig's head into thick slices and pan-sear with the olive oil in a frying pan over a medium heat for 4–5 minutes on each side until caramelized and beautifully crispy. Serve with the red cabbage salad.

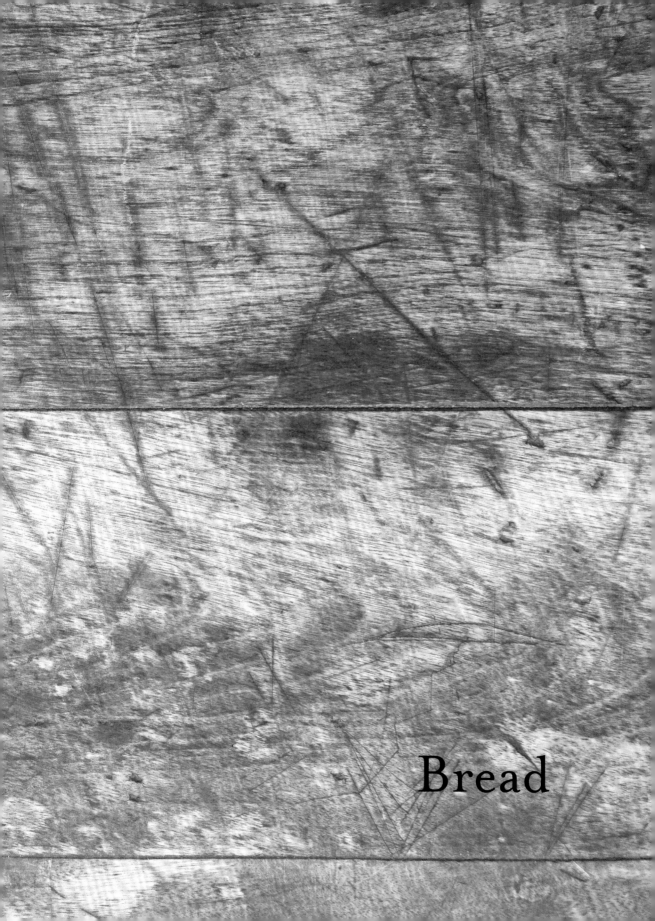

Bread

## Giselle

I don't agree with the idea that bread is bad for you. Good bread – not the plastic stuff – is a healthy, nourishing food and our family loves it.

When I was growing up my mother made all our bread. We ate lots of it as children, and I still eat it several times a day. When I first came to the UK in the late 1970s, I found that there wasn't much 'proper' bread available – just sliced white loaves in plastic bags. There were bakers but they all seemed to make the same loaf and there was certainly nothing that tasted like the bread I had grown up with. Things have changed, but back then the only thing for me to do was to make my own bread and I still do – three times a week. A lot of the recipes on the following pages are family favourites – things my mother used to make, including Baguettes (*see* page 236) and *Pain au Lait* (*see* page 243). Others are my own twists on classic breads, such as fougasse (*see* page 240) and rye bread (*see* page 232), that I have developed over the years.

When I bake bread I don't measure anything – I do it by eye and feel – so when writing the recipes for this book I had to measure everything very carefully, which I found quite tricky! Be prepared to adapt recipes when baking, as bread can vary according to the weather or the humidity on the day. Sometimes you may need less flour, or the dough may take longer to rise some days than on others. That's the magic of making bread.

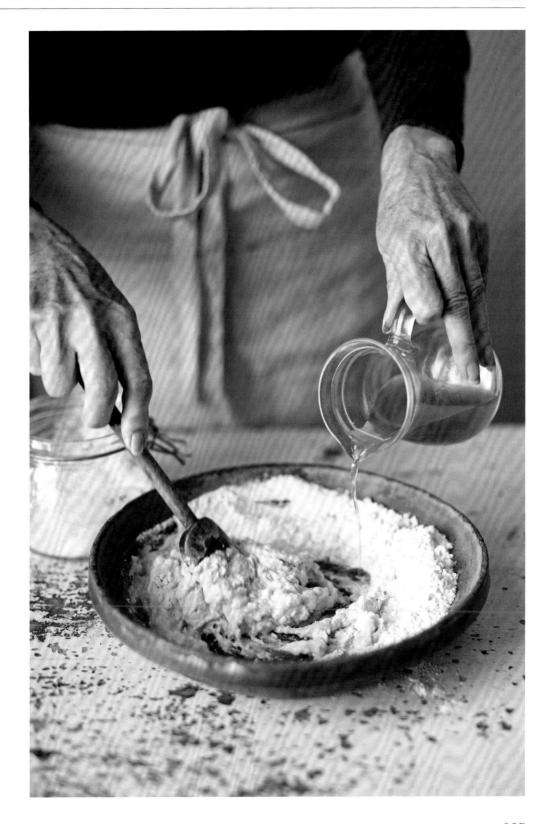

# Mother Dough

*It is so easy to make your own mother dough and keep it going for however long you like. Our own mother dough is nearly 5 years old and you can really tell the difference in flavour over time.*

### Makes 1 starter or mother dough

```
1 small bottle of beer
unbleached wheat flour
lukewarm water
```

Open the bottle of beer and leave it to settle for 5–6 days, until all the bubbles have dispersed and it is completely flat. Pour 150ml (¼ pint) of beer into a small mixing bowl and add 3 tablespoons of flour. Stir to combine (the mixture should achieve a creamy consistency), cover with something porous (such as muslin or a kitchen towel), then set aside in a warm place.

After approximately 3 days the mixture will begin to bubble and start to smell like yeast. At this stage, add another 4 tablespoons flour and 150ml (¼ pint) water. Stir to combine, then set aside in a warm place. From day 3 onwards, feed the dough with 2 tablespoons flour and 2 tablespoons water every other day.

On days 4 and 5, not much will appear to be happening and the mixture will look fairly lifeless. Don't be concerned – the bacteria contained in the mixture is beginning to die back, making way for the yeast to spring into action.

On day 6, 7 or 8 the mixture will suddenly come to life, doubling in volume after each feeding and releasing a yeasty aroma and lots of bubbles. This indicates that yeast is present and you now have a starter. At this stage you can store the starter in the fridge, but don't forget to feed it with an amount of flour and water equivalent to that removed every time you use some (so, for example, if you remove 120g/4½oz of the Mother Dough, feed it with 60g/2¼oz water and 60g/2¼oz flour).

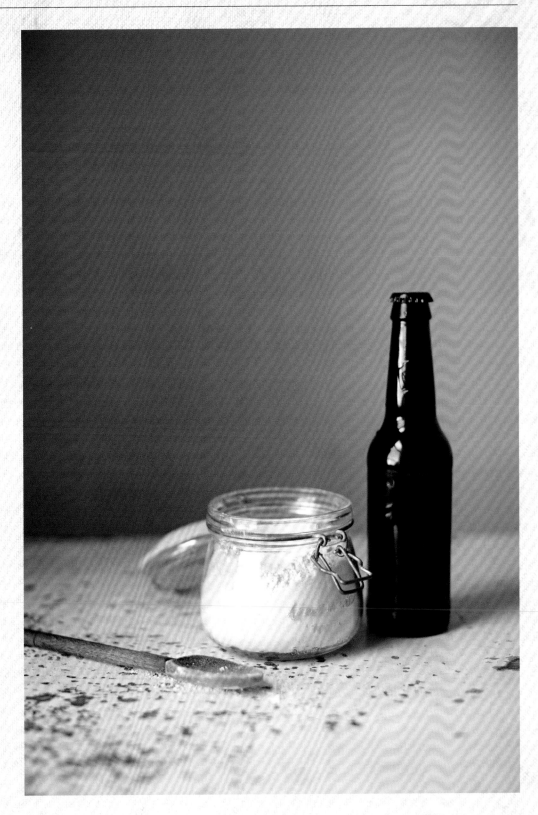

# Everyday Loaves

*This basic bread recipe is very versatile and can easily be adapted to include any nuts or dried fruit that you have to hand, making the end result even more special. Walnuts, pumpkin seeds, raisins or dried cranberries, or a combination of all of these, work especially well. Khorasan flour, also known as kamut flour, is a nutritious wholegrain flour with a slightly nutty flavour.*

**makes 2 × 900g (2lb) loaves**

butter, for greasing
90g (3¼oz) Mother Dough
  (see page 228)
100g (3½oz) white spelt
  flour
400g (14oz) Khorasan flour
400g (14oz) water
1 teaspoon fine sea salt
1 tablespoon runny honey
1 tablespoon Greek yogurt

Lightly grease 2 × 900g (2lb) loaf tins with butter.

Place all of the ingredients in a large bowl or the bowl of a stand mixer. Using your hands or the mixer, bring everything together to form a sticky dough. Continue to work the dough for 5 minutes, until smooth, then divide the mixture between the 2 loaf tins. Cover with cling film and set aside to rise at room temperature for up to a day, or until bubbles start to form in the dough. The time it takes to rise will vary depending on the weather, so check your dough every couple of hours to gauge its progress.

Twenty minutes before you want to bake your bread, preheat the oven to 240°C (475°F), Gas Mark 9 and place a roasting pan in the base of the oven.

Once the loaves have risen, remove the clingfilm and place the tins in the middle of the oven, adding a couple of glasses of cold water to the roasting pan at the base of the oven to create steam and help your bread rise. Bake for 15 minutes, then turn the oven down to 200°C (400°F), Gas Mark 6 and continue to bake for another 40 minutes, until the loaves sound hollow when tapped on their bases.

Leave the loaves to cool slightly in their tins before turning out and cooling to room temperature. The loaves are best eaten on the day of making.

# Irish Soda Bread

*This recipe is a joy because the dough doesn't need to rise, meaning that you can have fresh bread on the table within an hour of starting.*

**makes 2 × 900g (2lb) loaves**

butter, for greasing
375g (13oz) wholemeal flour
225g (8oz) self-raising
  flour
100g (3½oz) wheat bran
50g (1¾oz) jumbo porridge
  oats

70g (2½oz) pinhead
  porridge oats
15g (½oz) sea salt
2 teaspoons caster sugar
25g (1oz) bicarbonate
  of soda
1kg (2lb 4oz) buttermilk
20g (¾oz) black treacle

Preheat the oven to 200°C (400°F), Gas Mark 6 and lightly grease two 900g (2lb) loaf tins with butter.

Place all of the dry ingredients into the bowl of a stand mixer and whisk together to combine. Pour in the buttermilk and treacle and whisk on a low speed for 5 minutes, then turn the speed up to high and whisk for a further 2 minutes.

Divide the dough between the prepared loaf tins and transfer to the middle of the oven to bake for 50 minutes, until the loaves sound hollow when tapped on their bases. Turn the bread out of the tins and leave to cool on a wire rack before slicing.

# Rye Bread with Walnuts and Raisins

*This loaf doesn't need a lot of kneading, so can easily be made by hand. Rye flour produces a denser, darker and richer bread that is perfect for the colder seasons and makes a delicious accompaniment to warming winter soups.*

**makes 2 × 900g (2lb) loaves**

2 tablespoons olive oil,
  plus extra for greasing
230g (8¼oz) rye flour
350g (12oz) strong white
  bread flour
120g (4¼oz) Mother Dough
  (*see* page 228)
415g (14½oz) lukewarm
  water
75g (2¼oz) raisins
100g (3½oz) walnut halves
10g (¼oz) fine sea salt
1 teaspoon honey

Lightly grease 2 × 900g (2lb) loaf tins with olive oil.

Place all of the ingredients in a large bowl and, using your hands, bring everything together to form a sticky dough. Continue to work the dough for 5 minutes, until smooth, then divide the mixture between the 2 tins. Cover with clingfilm and set aside to rise at room temperature for up to a day, or until bubbles start to form in the dough. The time it takes to rise will vary depending on the weather, so check your dough every couple of hours to gauge its progress.

Twenty minutes before you want to bake your bread, preheat the oven to 240°C (475°F), Gas Mark 9 and place a roasting pan in the base of the oven.

Once the loaves have risen, remove the clingfilm and place the tins in the middle of the oven, adding a couple of glasses of cold water to the roasting pan at the base of the oven to create steam and help your bread rise. Bake for 15 minutes, then turn the oven down to 200°C (400°F), Gas Mark 6 and continue to bake for another 40 minutes, until the loaves sound hollow when tapped on their bases.

Leave the loaves to cool slightly in their tins before turning out and cooling to room temperature. The loaves are best eaten on the day of making.

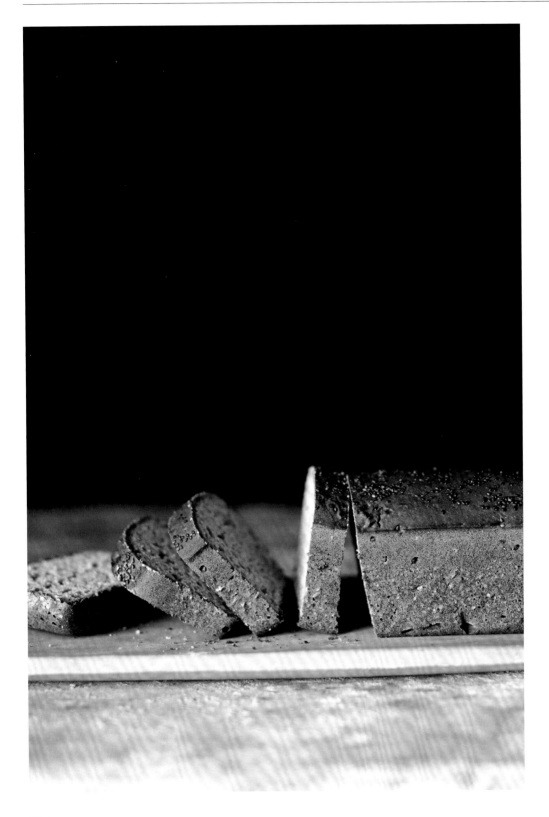

# Buckwheat Bread

*Traditionally used to make blinis, the flavoursome flour in this bread has a distinct taste and colour.*
*We have added a sprinkle of chia seeds on top for added 'nuttiness'.*

**makes 2 × 900g (2lb) loaves**

olive oil, for greasing
120g (4¼oz) Mother Dough
 (*see* page 228)
230g (8¼oz) buckwheat flour
300g (10½oz) strong white
 flour
430g (15oz) lukewarm water
10g (¼oz) sea salt
1 tablespoon honey
1 tablespoon goats' yogurt
 or Greek yogurt
chia seeds, for sprinkling

Lightly grease 2 × 900g (2lb) loaf tins with olive oil.

Place all of the ingredients in a large bowl and, using your hands, bring everything together to form a sticky dough. Continue to work the dough energetically for 5 minutes, until smooth (we tend to do this by hand but an electrical mixer could make the process a lot easier), then divide the mixture between the 2 tins. Cover with cling film and set aside to rise at room temperature for up to a day, or until bubbles start to form in the dough. The time it takes to rise will vary depending on the weather, so check your dough every couple of hours to gauge its progress.

Twenty minutes before you want to bake your bread, preheat the oven to 240°C (475°F), Gas Mark 9 and place a roasting pan in the base of the oven.

Once the loaves have risen, remove the clingfilm, sprinkle with chia seeds, and place the tins in the middle of the oven, adding a couple of glasses of cold water to the roasting pan at the base of the oven to create steam and help your bread rise. Bake for 20 minutes, then turn the oven down to 210°C (410°F), Gas Mark 6½ and continue to bake for another 20 minutes. Finally, take the loaves out of the oven, carefully remove them from their tins, then return them to the oven and bake for a further 5 minutes, until the loaves sound hollow when tapped on their bases.

Leave the loaves to cool to room temperature on a wire rack. Eat on the day of making or place in sealable plastic bags and keep in the fridge for several days.

# Baguettes

*Of all the French breads, the baguette is the most iconic and, with its perfect combination of deliciously crunchy crust and beautifully soft interior, it's not hard to see why.*

**makes 4 baguettes**

10g (¼oz) fresh yeast
375g (13oz) lukewarm water
500g (1lb 2oz) strong
  white flour, plus extra
  for flouring
12g (½oz) fine sea salt
olive oil, for greasing

Place the yeast in a small bowl with 2 tablespoons of the lukewarm water and stir until the yeast is completely dissolved.

Sift the flour into the bowl of a stand mixer fitted with a dough hook. Add the salt to the bowl and mix to distribute throughout the flour. Make a well in the centre of the flour and add three-quarters of the remaining water, followed by the dissolved yeast. With the mixer on a medium speed, leave to mix for 7 minutes, gradually adding the remaining water as the dough comes together. Once your dough is smooth and elastic transfer it to a lightly oiled bowl, cover with a clean kitchen towel, and set aside to rise at room temperature for 1½ hours, or until doubled in size. Meanwhile, line 2 large baking sheets with greaseproof paper.

Once the dough has risen, turn it out onto a lightly floured surface and knock back to remove any air bubbles. Divide the dough into 4 even-sized pieces and form each piece into a 30–35cm (12–14 inch) oblong. Place the baguettes on the prepared baking sheets and set aside to prove at room temperature for 1½ hours.

Preheat the oven to 230°C (450°F), Gas Mark 8.

Once the baguettes have proved, make several diagonal slashes on the top of each with a serrated knife and gently brush the tops with a little cold water. Transfer to the oven to bake for 25 minutes, until golden brown and crisp. Transfer to a wire rack to cool before slicing. These are best eaten the same day they are made.

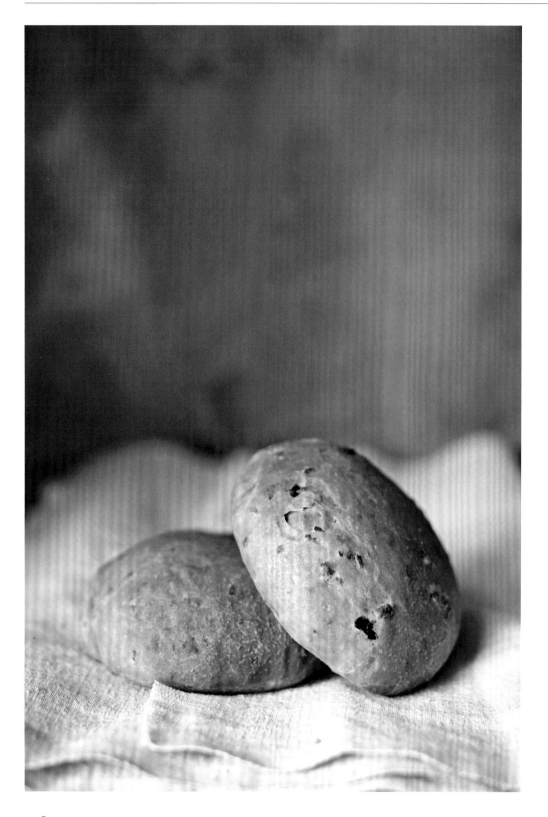

# Pan-bagnat with Sun-dried Tomatoes and Olives

*Pan-bagnat is a sandwich and street food speciality in Nice and Provence. The rolls are traditionally filled with the components of a classic Niçoise salad and eaten on the go, making them the perfect addition to any picnic.*

**makes 2 loaves**

600g (1lb 5oz) strong
  white flour, plus extra
  for dusting
10g (¼oz) fresh yeast
1 tablespoon olive oil,
  plus extra for greasing
400g (14oz) lukewarm
  water

2 teaspoons fine sea salt
75g (2¾oz) stoned green
  or black olives, roughly
  chopped
40g (1½oz) sundried
  tomatoes, roughly
  chopped

Sift the flour into a large bowl and add the yeast, crumbling it with your hands and rubbing it into the flour until you achieve a texture like fine breadcrumbs. Make a well in the centre of the flour mixture and pour in the olive oil and water. Using your hands, gradually bring the dry ingredients into the wet, then vigorously knead to form a sticky dough. Add the salt, olives and sundried tomatoes and mix again to distribute throughout the dough.

Turn the dough out onto a lightly floured work surface and knead vigorously for 5 minutes, until it is smooth and no longer sticky. Transfer the dough to a lightly oiled bowl, cover with a clean kitchen towel, and set aside to rise at room temperature for 1½ hours, or until doubled in size. Meanwhile, line 2 large baking sheets with greaseproof paper.

Once the dough has risen, turn it out onto a lightly floured work surface and knock back to remove any air bubbles. Divide the dough into 2 equal-sized pieces and shape each into a large, tight ball. Place the loaves on the prepared baking sheets and set aside to prove at room temperature, uncovered, for 1 hour.

Preheat the oven to 240°C (475°F), Gas Mark 9 and place a roasting pan in the base of the oven.

Once the dough has proved, transfer to the middle of the oven, adding a couple of glasses of cold water to the roasting pan at the base of the oven to create steam and help your bread rise. Bake for 10 minutes, then reduce the oven temperature to 190°C (375°F), Gas Mark 5 and bake for another 30 minutes, until golden brown and crisp. Transfer to a wire rack to cool before eating.

# Rosemary and Black Olive Fougasse

*This traditional and attractive southern French bread is usually made with crisped lardons or black olives. This is delicious eaten as it is, but spread with tapenade and anchoïade (see page 96) it makes a perfect pre-dinner snack.*

**makes 1 fougasse**

150g (5½oz) strong white flour, plus extra for dusting
100g (3½oz) self-raising flour

6g (⅛oz) fresh yeast
2 tablespoons olive oil, plus extra for greasing
150g (5oz) lukewarm water
1 teaspoon fine sea salt

40g (1½oz) stoned black olives, roughly chopped
½ rosemary sprig, leaves chopped

Sift both flours into a large bowl and add the yeast, crumbling it with your hands and rubbing into the flour until you achieve a texture like fine breadcrumbs. Make a well in the centre of the flour mixture and pour in the olive oil and water. Using your hands, gradually bring the dry ingredients into the wet, then vigorously knead to form a sticky dough. Add the salt, olives and rosemary to the dough and mix again to distribute throughout the dough.

Turn the dough out onto a lightly floured work surface and knead vigorously for 5 minutes, or until it is smooth and no longer sticky. Transfer the dough to a lightly oiled bowl and set aside to rise at room temperature, covered with a clean kitchen towel, for 1½ hours, or until doubled in size. Meanwhile, line a 30 × 20cm (12 × 8 inch) baking sheet with greaseproof paper.

Once the dough has risen, turn it out onto a lightly floured work surface and knock back to remove any air bubbles. Roll or press your dough out to form a large rectangle, roughly the size of your prepared baking sheet. Transfer the dough to your baking

sheet and press the dough again to fill right up to the edges. Using a sharp knife, make a long vertical incision down the centre of the fougasse, leaving the dough intact at the top and bottom. Now make 3 diagonal slashes on either side of the central slash. Once finished the bread should resemble a leaf. Lightly brush the fougasse with olive oil and set aside to prove at room temperature, uncovered, for 1 hour.

Preheat the oven to 230°C (450°F), Gas Mark 8 and place a roasting pan in the base of the oven.

Once the dough has proved, place it in the middle of the oven, adding a couple of glasses of cold water to the roasting pan at the base of the oven to create steam and help your bread rise. Bake for 8 minutes, then reduce the oven temperature to 200°C (400°F), Gas Mark 6 and bake for another 10 minutes, until golden brown and crisp. Transfer to a wire rack to cool before eating. This is best eaten the same day it is made.

# Pizza Dough

*Whatever toppings you and your family prefer, the key to a good pizza is a thin and crispy base. This recipe makes enough for four large pizzas, but you can portion and freeze the dough before proving for use at a later date.*

**makes 4 × 30cm (12 inches) pizza bases**

1kg (2lb 4oz) plain flour
30g (1oz) fresh yeast
100g (3½oz) olive oil,
 plus extra for greasing
600g (1lb 5oz) lukewarm
 water
20g (¾oz) fine sea salt

Place the flour, yeast, olive oil and 400g (14oz) of the water in the bowl of a stand mixer fitted with a dough hook. Beat on a medium speed for at least 2 minutes until the dough begins to form a ball.

Dissolve the salt in the remaining water and pour gradually into the dough until it is all incorporated, then leave to mix for 5–10 minutes, until the dough has formed a smooth ball. Transfer the dough to a lightly oiled bowl and cover with a damp kitchen towel. Set aside to rise at room temperature for 2 hours, or until the dough has doubled in size.

Once the dough has risen, turn it out onto a lightly floured bowl or surface and divide it into 4 equal-sized pieces. Roll each piece out

to form a 30cm (12 inch) round, about 5mm (¼ inch) thick. Transfer to a floured pizza or baking tray and set aside to prove at room temperature for 30 minutes.

Preheat the oven to 220°C (425°F), Gas Mark 7.

Once the dough has proved, add your toppings and transfer to the oven to bake for 10 minutes, then reduce the oven temperature to 200°C (400°F), Gas Mark 6 and cook for another 10 minutes. Serve the pizzas hot.

# Pain au Lait

*These small brioche-like rolls are perfect for weekend mornings when you
have a little time to sit and relax over breakfast. They are deliciously soft and
light and make the ideal accompaniment to homemade jams and preserves.*

**makes 25 small rolls**

480g (1lb 1oz) plain flour,
 plus extra for flouring
15g (½oz) granulated sugar
1 teaspoon fine sea salt
50g (1¾oz) butter, cubed
340g (11¾oz) whole milk
15g (½oz) fresh yeast
2 egg yolks, beaten

Sift the flour into a large bowl, then add the
sugar and salt and mix to combine. Add the
cubed butter to the bowl and, using your hands,
rub the butter into the flour until the mixture
looks like fine breadcrumbs. Set aside.

Place the milk and yeast in a small pan over a
low heat. Mix until the yeast has dissolved into
the milk and the liquid is warm, but not hot.

Make a well in the centre of the dry
ingredients and pour in the milk, then use
your hands to bring everything together to
a sticky dough. Turn the dough out onto a
lightly floured work surface and knead for
around 5 minutes, until smooth and elastic.
Transfer the dough to a lightly floured bowl
and set aside to rise at room temperature,
covered, for 1 hour, or until doubled in size.
Meanwhile, line 2 large baking trays with
greaseproof paper.

Once the dough has risen, turn it out onto
a lightly floured work surface and knock back
to remove any air bubbles. Divide the dough
into 25 equal-sized pieces and roll into tight
balls in the cupped palms of your hands.
Transfer the shaped dough to the prepared
baking trays, leaving enough space between
each to allow them to expand. Set aside to
prove at room temperature for 1 hour, or
until almost doubled in size.

Preheat the oven to 200°C (400°F), Gas
Mark 6.

Brush the tops of the rolls with the egg
yolk and transfer to the oven to bake for
10–15 minutes, until golden and well risen.
Transfer to a wire rack to cool.

# Chocolate-filled Brioche

*The dough for these brioche is prepared the night before baking and then left to prove slowly in the fridge overnight, meaning that they can be on the table quickly the next morning for an indulgent and impressive weekend breakfast.*

**makes 10 small brioche**

250g (9oz) plain flour
7g (¼oz) fresh yeast
100g (3½oz) whole milk
4 tablespoons granulated
  sugar
seeds from 1 vanilla pod
2 egg yolks
1 teaspoon fine sea salt

125g (4½oz) butter, cubed,
  at room temperature,
  plus extra for greasing
125g (4½oz) dark chocolate
  (at least 70 percent
  cocoa solids), broken
  into cubes
1 egg, beaten

The evening before you bake the brioche, sift the flour into the bowl of a stand mixer fitted with a dough hook. Add the yeast and mix at a slow speed for 2 minutes to combine.

Place the milk, sugar and vanilla seeds in a small pan over a medium heat. Heat until the sugar has dissolved and the milk has just warmed. Take off the heat and whisk the egg yolks into the pan.

Make a well in the centre of the flour and yeast mixture and pour in the milk and egg mixture, followed by the salt. With the mixer at a medium speed, mix for around 5 minutes, until the dough has formed into a smooth ball. With the mixer still running, add the butter a cube at a time until it is all incorporated into the dough. Transfer the dough to a lightly floured bowl, cover with clingfilm and transfer to the fridge to rise overnight.

The next morning, preheat the oven to 200°C (400°F), Gas Mark 6 and grease a muffin tin with butter.

Remove the risen dough from the fridge and divide into 10 equal-sized pieces. On a floured surface, press each of the dough pieces out flat and place a cube of the chocolate in the centre. Bring the edges of the dough up to enclose the chocolate and pinch together to seal. Using the cupped palms of your hands, form the chocolate-filled dough pieces into ball shapes and transfer to the prepared muffin tin. Brush the tops of the brioches with beaten egg and transfer to the oven to bake for 15–20 minutes, until golden and well risen.

Immediately turn the brioches out of the tin and leave to cool slightly on a wire rack. Serve warm, with the chocolate melted and oozy in the centre.

# Preserves, Pickles and Pâtés

# Giselle

As my family grew most of our food, there were
times of the year when we inevitably had gluts
of certain ingredients. We'd have more peas,
beans, tomatoes or apricots than we could eat.
Nothing could be wasted and we had no freezer in
those days, so my mother would preserve whatever
she could. Her storeroom was lined with jar upon
jar of preserved vegetables to use throughout the
winter months. She would bottle lovely ripe fruit,
make jam and cook up huge batches of tasty tomato
and basil sauce that we would enjoy all year
round. We would all help, of course. When peas
were in season, for instance, my father would
unload mountains of them onto the kitchen table
for us to pod. The first one to fill their bowl
would be let off washing up that night, making
it a fiercely contested competition.

I love preserving and still more or less follow
my mother's methods.

Sterilize each pickle or preserve jar and lid
by washing them thoroughly in hot, soapy water,
running them through a dishwasher or placing
them in a large pan of simmering water for about
5–10 minutes. Remove with tongs and leave to
drain and dry before filling and water-bath
canning, if required (*see* page 251).

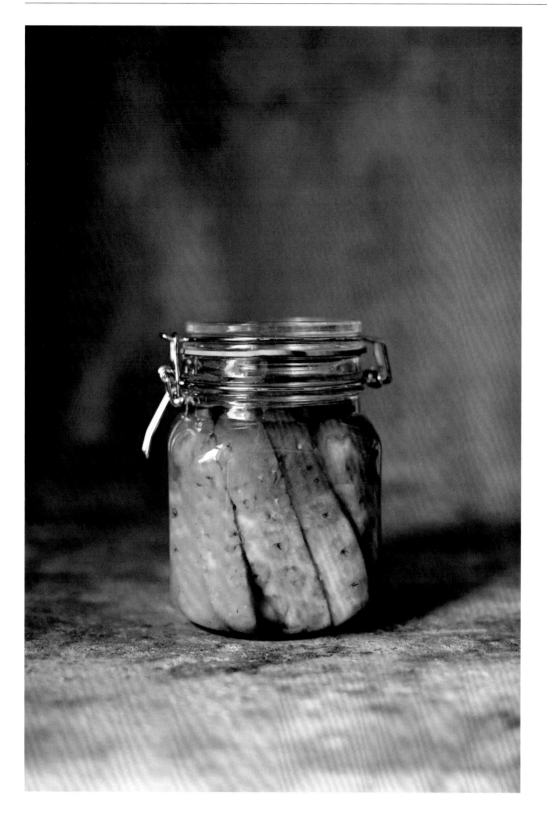

# Sweet Preserves

*Here are a few guidelines to follow when making sweet preserves at home.*

## For Fruits in Syrup:

Light fruits (e.g. plums):
  1 litre (1¾ pints) water to 250g
  (9oz) sugar
Medium-weight fruits (e.g. peaches):
  1 litre (1¾ pints) water to 350g
  (12oz) sugar
Heavy fruits (e.g. pineapple):
  1 litre (1¾ pints) water to 650g
  (1lb 7oz) sugar

## Pineapple in Syrup

**fills a 1 litre (1¾ pint) jar**

1 pineapple
650g (1lb 7oz) caster sugar
1 litre (1¾ pints) water

Peel, halve and core the pineapple. Slice each pineapple half into 3 even wedges, then reconstruct the fruit and place in a large sterilized jar (*see* page 248). Place the sugar and water in large pan over a high heat and bring just to the boil. Pour the liquid over the pineapple up to the brim of the jar and seal.

For the water-bath canning, line a large saucepan with cardboard, a kitchen towel or kitchen paper and fill with water. Bring to a gentle simmer. Place the sealed jar inside, topping up with boiling water if necessary to ensure the lid is covered by 1cm (½ inch). Simmer for 30 minutes then remove from the heat, leaving the jar in the saucepan to cool completely before removing and storing.

Store for up to 1 year in a cool place. Once opened, store in the fridge and use within 1 month.

## Plums in Syrup

**fills a 1 litre (1¾ pint) jar**

500g (1lb 2oz) plums, stoned
  and quartered
seeds of 1 vanilla pod
1 litre (1¾ pints) water
250g (9oz) caster sugar

Place the plums and vanilla seeds in a large sterilized jar (*see* page 248) and set aside. Place the sugar and water in a large pan over a high heat and bring just to the boil. Pour the liquid over the plums up to the brim of the jar and seal. Process following the water-bath canning instructions (*see* left). Store for up to 1 year in a cool place. Once opened, store in the fridge and use within 1 month.

# Apple Compote

### fills a 650ml (22fl oz) jar

800g (1lb 12oz) cox apples, peeled,
  cored and roughly chopped
2 tablespoons lemon juice
25g (1oz) golden caster sugar
1 pinch of ground cinnamon

Place the apples, lemon juice and caster sugar in a large pan over a medium heat. Bring to a simmer, then cover the pan and cook over a low heat for 25 minutes, until soft and golden. Transfer the mixture to a blender with a pinch of cinnamon and blend until completely smooth. Transfer to a sterilized jar (*see* page 248) and seal. Process for 25 minutes following the water-bath canning instructions (*see* page 251). This can be eaten warm or cooled. Once opened, store in the fridge and use within 1 month.

# White Peach Jam with Cordial

### fills a 800ml (27fl oz) jar

1kg (2lb 4oz) white peaches, stoned
  and roughly chopped
400g (14oz) caster sugar
3 tablespoons elderflower cordial

Place the peaches, sugar and cordial in a large pan over a medium heat. Bring to the boil, then reduce the heat to a simmer and cook for 20 minutes, stirring frequently. If you prefer a smooth jam, place in a blender and blend until smooth before transferring to a sterilized jar (*see* page 248) and sealing. Process for 25 minutes following the water-bath canning instructions (*see* page 251). Store unopened for up to 1 year in a cool place. Once opened, store in the fridge and use within 1 month.

# Quince Pâte de Fruit

*Emily: My grandmother has always made delicious quince pâte. This is her precious recipe.*

**fills a 900g (2lb) cake tin**

1kg (2lb 4oz) quince,
  peeled, cored and
  quartered
750g (1lb 10oz) caster
  sugar, plus extra for
  coating
seeds of 1 vanilla pod

Line a large round or rectangular cake tin or lipped baking sheet with greaseproof paper and set aside until needed.

Place the quince in a large pan over a medium heat with enough water to just cover the fruit. Bring to a boil, then reduce the heat to a simmer and cook for 25 minutes, until tender.

Drain the fruit and transfer to a blender, then blend until completely smooth.

Return the purée to the pan along with the sugar and vanilla seeds and cook over a medium heat, stirring continuously, until the sugar has dissolved and the mixture has started to bubble.

Turn the heat down to a gentle simmer and cook, stirring occasionally, for 30–40 minutes, until the mixture has thickened and darkened to a deep orange colour. Pour the mixture into your prepared cake tin or baking sheet and leave to cool and set.

This can then be cut into pieces and rolled in sugar to be enjoyed as a sweet snack or left as it is for use with savoury dishes. Store in the fridge and use within 1 year.

# Savoury Preserves

## Preserved Peas

**fills a 1 litre (1¾ pint) jar**

2kg (4lb 8oz) fresh peas, shelled
1 litre (1¾ pints) water, plus extra
  for boiling peas
20g (¾oz) salt

Bring a large pan of water to the boil, add the peas and blanch for 4 minutes, until tender. Rinse immediately in iced water, then drain. Transfer the cooked and cooled peas to a large sterilized jar (*see* page 248) and set aside. Place the water and salt in a large pan over a high heat, bring to the boil, then immediately pour the liquid over the peas and seal. Process following the water-bath canning instructions (*see* page 251). Store unopened for up to 1 year in a cool place. Once opened, store in the fridge and use within 1 month.

## Preserved Runner Beans

**fills a 1 litre (1¾ pint) jar**

1kg (2lb 4oz) fresh runner beans, trimmed
1 litre (1¼ pints) water, plus extra for
  boiling beans
20g (¾oz) salt

Bring a large pan of water to the boil, add the beans and blanch until tender. Rinse immediately in iced water, then drain. Transfer the cooked and cooled beans to a large sterilized jar (*see* page 248) and set aside.

Place the water and salt in a large pan over a high heat, bring to the boil, then immediately pour the liquid over the beans and seal. Process following the water-bath canning instructions (*see* page 251). Store unopened for up to 1 year in a cool place. Once opened, store in the fridge and use within 1 month.

## Artichokes in Vinegar

**fills a 500ml (18fl oz) jar**

250ml (9fl oz) water
250ml (9fl oz) white wine vinegar
juice of ½ lemon
10-15 small artichoke hearts
10 black peppercorns
1 small bay leaf
250ml (9fl oz) olive oil
salt

Place the water, white wine vinegar, lemon juice and a pinch of salt in a large pan over a medium heat. Bring just to the boil then add the artichoke hearts and cook until tender, approximately 12 minutes. Strain the artichokes, discarding the cooking liquid, and set aside to dry on a clean kitchen towel. Once dry, place the artichokes in a sterilized jar (*see* page 248) with the peppercorns and bay leaf, then top up the jar with the olive oil and seal. Process following the water-bath canning instructions (*see* page 251). Store unopened for up to 1 year in a cool place. Once opened, store in the fridge and use within 1 month.

# Tomato and Basil Sauce

*Giselle: I think it's safe to say on behalf of all my siblings that the tomato season was by far the worst time of year when we were children. The whole family seemed always to be covered head-to-toe with tomato juice and seeds as preserving our crop was a shared task and took several, messy days.*

### fills a 1 litre (1¾ pint) jar

2 tablespoons olive oil
1 onion, finely chopped
2 garlic cloves, finely chopped
2kg (4lb 8oz) ripe tomatoes
1 thyme sprig
½ bunch of basil, leaves ripped
½ teaspoon dried chilli flakes
1 pinch of caster sugar
salt and freshly ground black pepper

Place the olive oil in a wide shallow pan over a medium heat. Once hot, add the onion and garlic and cook, stirring continuously, for 3 minutes, until soft and translucent. Add the rest of the ingredients to the pan and season to taste. Bring to a gentle simmer and leave to cook for 30 minutes, until reduced by half. Transfer to a sterilized jar (*see* page 248) and seal. Process following the water-bath canning instructions (*see* page 251). This can be used as it is for a pasta sauce or blended until smooth to make a great tomato base for pizzas. Once opened, store in the fridge and use within 1 month.

# Chicken Liver Pâté

*Giselle: Chicken liver pâté is a great favourite of Emily's and is something my mother would make and store. She hated waste and would always be sure to use up any chicken livers. This is delicious spread thickly over toasted baguette.*

### fills 2 × 350ml (12fl oz) jars

200g (7oz) butter, softened
500g (1lb 2oz) trimmed chicken livers
3 shallots, finely chopped
1 thyme sprig
100ml (3½fl oz) port
50ml (2fl oz) cognac
salt and freshly ground black pepper

Heat 1 tablespoon of the butter in a frying pan over a medium heat. Once melted and bubbling, add the chicken livers, shallots and thyme sprig and sauté for 3–4 minutes, depending on size. Deglaze the pan with the port and reduce by half. Transfer to a bowl and set aside to cool to room temperature. Once cooled, transfer the mixture to a blender and blend until smooth, gradually incorporating the remaining butter and the cognac. Once smooth and fully incorporated, season the pâté to taste and transfer the mixture to 2 sterilized jars (*see* page 248) and seal. Place in the fridge overnight to set. Store in the fridge and use within 3 days.

# Classic Desserts

## Emily

A family dinner doesn't feel complete unless
it ends with something sweet. Even following the
heaviest of meals, after a little break, there's
always room for a little something. When we're
on holiday in France, we always take plenty of
time to talk and laugh over dinner and have a
dessert every day.

Cakes and desserts bring our whole family
together and all three of us love simple
old-fashioned dishes the best. For all the new
ingredients and techniques we've embraced in
our cooking, we always come back to traditional
recipes when it comes to the sweet course. Our
*beignets* (*see* page 274), clafoutis (*see* page
286) and fruit tarts (*see* page 287) taste
exactly like those my grandmother used to
cook and are perfect just the way they are.

There are some exceptions, though. I've
discovered that aubergines are a wonderful,
if unlikely, addition to chocolate pots
(*see* page 293), adding texture and interest;
Oreos give a wonderfully contemporary twist to
classic Spanish doughnuts (*see* page 268); and
my feather-light *Gâteau de Savoie* (*see* page 264)
is lighter than the version that my mother
used to eat as a child.

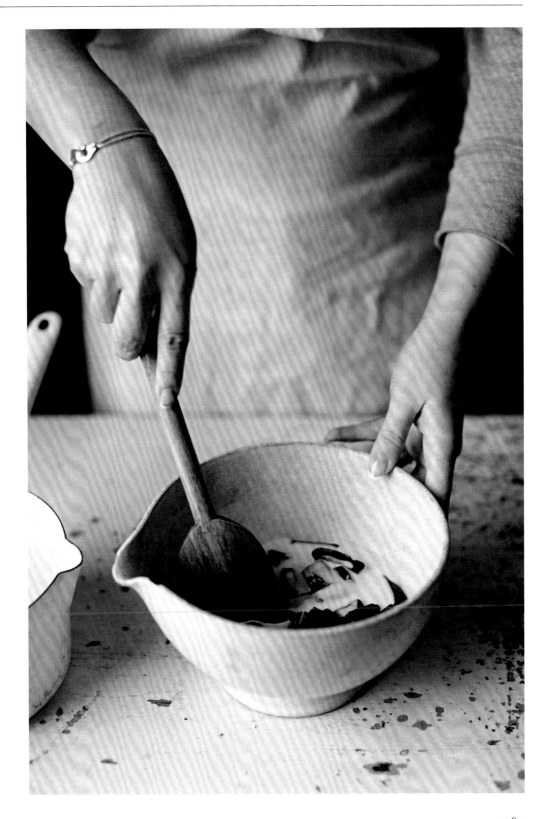

# Gâteau de Savoie

*This is an extremely light and airy cake that is delicious with tea and coffee, toasted at breakfast time or served with clotted cream.*

**serves 8**

60g (2¼oz) unsalted
  butter, melted, plus
  extra for greasing
225g (8oz) caster sugar
210g (7½oz) egg whites

140g (5oz) egg yolks
80g (2¾oz) cornflour
80g (2¾oz) plain flour
1½ teaspoons baking powder
clotted cream, to serve

Preheat the oven to 160°C (325°F), Gas Mark 3 and grease the inside of a deep 20cm (8 inch) round cake tin with melted butter. Sprinkle 15g (½oz) of the sugar over the surface of the tin and set aside.

Place the egg whites in a large mixing bowl or the bowl of a stand mixer and whisk to firm peaks. With the whisk still running, gradually add 120g (4½oz) of the sugar to form a smooth, glossy meringue. Set aside.

In another bowl, whisk the egg yolks with the remaining sugar, until pale and thickened. Pour this mixture into the egg white mixture and carefully fold the two mixtures together until just combined. It is very important to be gentle here – if you are too vigorous you will knock the air out of your mixture and end up with a flat, dense cake.

Sift the cornflour, flour and baking powder over the egg mixture, then carefully fold them through until combined. Pour the mixture into your prepared cake tin and transfer to the oven to cook for 35 minutes, until well risen, golden and springy to the touch.

Set the cake aside for 10 minutes before removing it from the tin. The cake is delicious served warm or cold with clotted cream.

# Classic Honey Madeleines

*Dainty, bite-sized madeleines make a delicious tea-time treat or gift. In France, the family madeleine recipe is a closely guarded secret, but we are sharing ours with you here.*

**makes 60 madeleines**

85g (3oz) egg yolks
300g (10½oz) beaten egg
seeds of 1 vanilla pod
250g (9oz) caster sugar
250g (9oz) plain flour,
  plus extra for flouring

2½ teaspoons baking
  powder
15g (½oz) good-quality
  runny honey
300g (10½oz) unsalted
  clarified butter
1½ teaspoons salt
butter, for greasing

The day before you want to bake the madeleines, whisk the egg yolks, beaten eggs and vanilla seeds together in a large mixing bowl. Add the sugar and continue to beat until pale and foamy. Sift the flour, baking powder and salt into the bowl and carefully fold in until just incorporated. Melt the honey and clarified butter together in the microwave, then pour into the madeleine batter and stir until just combined. Cover with clingfilm and transfer to the fridge overnight.

The next day, preheat your oven to 230°C (450°F), Gas Mark 8 and butter and flour your madeleine moulds (if you are using silicone moulds, they will not need to be greased). The easiest way to fill the moulds with the batter is by using a disposable piping bag without a nozzle, but a tablespoon will also work well. Fill each mould to around the halfway level, being as even as you can.

To cook the madeleines perfectly, you need to use a timer. Transfer the madeleines to the oven to cook for 3 minutes, then turn off the oven for a further 2 minutes. Finally, turn the oven on again at 180°C (350°F), Gas Mark 4 and leave to cook for another 10 minutes, turning the tray halfway through the cooking time, until well risen and golden. Turning the oven off and then on again creates the bumps in the middles of the madeleines.

Leave the madeleines to cool for 10 minutes in their tins before turning out. Do not let them cool entirely in their tins as they will stick and be impossible to remove cleanly. These are best eaten on the day they are made.

# Oreo Churros with Coconut and Vanilla Chantilly

*This modern take on the classic Spanish doughnuts will be a hit with young and old alike. The coconut Chantilly also makes an excellent icing and has the added bonus of being dairy free.*

**serves 4–6**

**For the coconut Chantilly:**
1 × 400ml (14fl oz) can
  full-fat coconut milk
seeds of 1 vanilla pod
1 teaspoon runny honey

**For the Oreo churros:**
15 Oreo cookies
1 tablespoon caster sugar
240ml (8½fl oz) water
1 teaspoon salt
30g (1oz) unsalted butter
60g (2¼oz) plain flour,
  sifted
1 egg

neutral oil, such as
  rapeseed or sunflower,
  for shallow frying

**For the sugar coating:**
1 tablespoon ground
  cinnamon
2 tablespoons caster sugar

Start preparing the coconut Chantilly the day before you want to serve the churros. Pour the coconut milk into a bowl and place in the fridge overnight. The next day the milk should have separated into a thick cream and a thin milk. Drain off the milk (this can be used to make smoothies) and place the remaining cream in a large mixing bowl. Using an electric whisk, whisk the coconut cream for 3 minutes, until light and fluffy. Stir in the vanilla seeds and honey and set aside in the fridge until ready to use.

To make the churros, separate the 2 halves of each Oreo and scrape out and discard the filling. Place the dark shells in a food processor and process to a fine black powder. Set aside.

Place the sugar, water, salt and butter in a large pan over a medium heat. When the butter has melted and the liquid has just started to boil, remove the pan from the heat and tip in the flour and black Oreo powder. Mix thoroughly with a wooden spoon until the mixture forms a ball and pulls away cleanly from the sides of the pan. Add the egg to the mixture and continue to beat until you obtain a smooth paste.

Line a baking sheet that will fit in your freezer with greaseproof paper and fill a piping bag fitted with a large star-shaped nozzle with the churros mixture. Pipe straight 10cm (4 inch) churros onto the baking sheet until all of the mixture is used up. Transfer the baking sheet to the freezer for around 30 minutes, until the churros are firm enough to lift off the greaseproof paper by hand.

Meanwhile, combine the ingredients for the sugar coating in a small bowl and set aside until needed.

Around 10 minutes before you want to start frying, half fill a frying pan with oil. Heat the oil to a temperature of 185°C (365°F) then, working in small batches, carefully lower the churros into the oil and cook for 6 minutes, turning halfway through cooking. The churros should be crispy and golden on the outside with a light fluffy centre. Transfer the cooked churros to kitchen paper to drain off any excess oil, then roll in the sugar coating whilst still hot.

Serve the churros warm with the coconut Chantilly alongside for dipping.

# Beignets aux Pommes

*These deliciously warming apple fritters are perfect for winter days when you want to wrap up and hunker down inside to escape the cold.*

**serves 4**

250ml (9fl oz) whole milk
1 vanilla pod, halved and
  seeds removed
150g (5½oz) plain flour
1½ teaspoons baking powder
2 egg yolks
2 tablespoons vegetable
  or sunflower oil

15g (½oz) caster sugar
3–4 apples ('Golden
  Delicious' or 'Pink
  Lady' work well),
  peeled, cored and cut
  into 5mm (¼ inch) slices
sunflower or corn oil, for
  deep-frying
icing sugar, for dusting

Place the milk in a medium pan over a low heat. Add the vanilla pod and seeds to the pan and leave on the heat until just starting to simmer. Do not allow the milk to boil. Remove the pan from the heat and set aside until lukewarm for the flavours to infuse.

Meanwhile, sift the flour and baking powder into a large mixing bowl, then add the egg yolks, oil and caster sugar. Discard the vanilla pod from the milk, then gradually whisk the milk into the flour and egg mixture until fully incorporated. If you have any lumps, continue to whisk until you have a smooth liquid batter. Cover the mixture with clingfilm and set aside to rest for 1 hour in the fridge.

Around 15 minutes before you want to start frying, heat your oil to 180°C (350°F). If using a deep-fat fryer use the amount recommended by the manufacturer (most domestic varieties vary between 1–3 litres/ 1¾–5¼ pints); if using a deep pan, 1.5 litres (2½ pints) should be sufficient. The oil needs to be around 10cm (4 inches) deep, but nowhere near the top lip of the pan.

When the oil is up to temperature, dip batches of the apple slices in the batter and then carefully transfer them to the hot oil. Be careful not to overload your fryer or pan as the fritters will not cook evenly. Cook for 5 minutes, turning the slices over halfway through the cooking time. Transfer the cooked fritters to a plate lined with kitchen paper to drain off any excess oil while you cook the remainder of the apple slices.

Once all of the fritters are cooked, dust generously with icing sugar and serve warm.

# Brioche and Butter Pudding

*This is a simple recipe that the whole family will enjoy. It is a great way to use up any leftover bread you have in the house and you can substitute the brioche with whatever you have to hand — croissants or panettone work well, but result in a slightly richer pudding. Nutmeg, cinnamon or chopped nuts also make a welcome addition.*

**serves 4**

30g (1oz) raisins
1 tablespoon dark rum
180ml (6¼fl oz) whole milk
3 eggs
100g (3½oz) caster sugar,
  plus extra for
  sprinkling
seeds of 1 vanilla pod
240g (8½oz) sliced brioche
15g (½oz) unsalted
  butter, diced, plus
  extra for greasing

Preheat the oven to 190°C (375°F), Gas Mark 5 and grease a round 20cm (8 inch) baking dish with butter.

Place the raisins in a small bowl and pour over the rum. Set aside to macerate while you prepare the rest of the dish.

Place the milk in a small pan over a low heat. Bring just to the boil, then immediately remove from the heat. Set aside for a couple of minutes to cool slightly.

Meanwhile, place the eggs, sugar and vanilla seeds in a large mixing bowl and whisk until pale and frothy. Once the milk has cooled

slightly (if it is too hot it will scramble the eggs), gradually pour it into the egg mixture, constantly whisking, until fully combined. Working one slice at a time, dip the brioche into the custard and leave to soak for around a minute. Neatly arrange the soaked brioche in your prepared baking dish, ensuring it is well filled with no gaps.

Pour the rum and raisin mixture into the custard and then pour this whole mixture over the top of your arranged brioche. Scatter a little sugar over the pudding and dot the cubes of butter over the top. Transfer to the oven to bake for 40–45 minutes, until golden brown and crisp. Serve hot.

# Mini-Cannelés Bordelais

*This is a speciality of the region of Bordeaux, very often served with coffee, but equally delicious served as a pudding with ice cream or crème anglaise alongside. The batter needs to be made a day ahead, but if you're organized they are more than worth the effort.*

**makes 60** *mini-cannelés*

500ml (18fl oz) whole milk
50g (1¾oz) unsalted
  butter, plus extra for
  greasing
1 vanilla pod, halved and
  seeds removed

200g (7oz) caster sugar
2 eggs and 2 egg yolks
100g (3½oz) plain flour
1 tablespoon dark rum
pinch of salt
crème anglaise (*see* page
  293) or ice cream,
  to serve (optional)

The day before you want to serve the *cannelés*, place the milk in a large pan over a low heat. Add the butter and vanilla pod and seeds and leave on the heat until the butter has just melted. Do not allow the milk to boil. Once the butter has melted into the milk, remove the pan from the heat and set aside for a few minutes for the flavours to infuse.

Meanwhile, place the sugar, eggs and egg yolks in a large mixing bowl and whisk until pale. Sift the flour into the mixture, then add the rum and a pinch of salt and mix to combine.

Remove the vanilla pods from the milk mixture and discard. Whisking all the time, gradually pour the lukewarm milk into the flour and egg mixture until fully incorporated. If there are any lumps, continue to whisk until you have a smooth liquid batter. Cover the mixture with clingfilm and transfer to the fridge overnight.

The next day, preheat your oven to 260°C (500°F), Gas Mark 10 and grease your *mini-cannelés* moulds with butter (if you are using silicone moulds, they won't need to be greased).

Remove the batter mixture from the fridge and stir briefly to ensure it is well combined. Pour the batter mixture into the moulds, stopping just short of the top to allow a little room for the *cannelés* to rise during cooking.

Transfer the *cannelés* to the oven and cook for 8 minutes, then immediately reduce the temperature to 180°C (350°F), Gas Mark 4 and leave to cook for a further 40 minutes, until the tops are dark brown and crisp to the touch. Set aside to cool for at least 10 minutes.

Once they have cooled slightly, remove the *cannelés* from their moulds and serve warm with crème anglaise or ice cream alongside, if liked.

# Hazelnut and Blueberry Cookies

*A good cookie recipe is a must for any cook: they can be thrown together quickly, travel well and everyone loves them. You could even portion the dough and freeze it for baking off at a moment's notice.*

**makes 25 cookies**

175g (6oz) unsalted
  butter, softened
100g (3½oz) demerara sugar
50g (1¾oz) caster sugar
2 eggs, beaten
2 teaspoons vanilla
  extract
250g (9oz) large rolled
  oats

160g (5¾oz) dried
  blueberries
125g (4½oz) chopped
  hazelnuts, lightly
  toasted
125g (4½oz) plain flour
1 teaspoon bicarbonate
  of soda
½ teaspoon salt

Preheat the oven to 180°C (350°F), Gas Mark 4 and line 2 or 3 large baking sheets with greaseproof paper.

In a large bowl, cream the butter and both sugars together until light and creamy. Add the eggs and vanilla extract and beat until well combined. Add the oats, blueberries and hazelnuts and stir to combine. Finally, sift over the flour and bicarbonate of soda and add the salt. Mix until everything is well combined and the ingredients are evenly distributed.

Using your hands or an ice-cream scoop, divide the mixture into 20 even-sized balls. Lay the balls on your prepared baking trays and press them down slightly with your fingertips to form cookie shapes. These will spread during cooking, so don't place them too close to each other. If you don't have enough baking trays or your oven is small, you will need to bake in batches.

Transfer the cookies to the oven to bake for 10–15 minutes, depending on how soft you like your cookies. Transfer to a wire rack to cool and serve warm or at room temperature.

# Rice Pudding

*This classic dessert is a guaranteed crowd pleaser and very simple to prepare. If you are lucky enough to own a wood-fired oven, the smoky taste imparted by the embers will add an extra layer of flavour that will be sure to surprise and delight your guests.*

**serves 4**

600ml (20fl oz) whole milk
70g (2½oz) pudding rice
30g (1oz) caster sugar
1 pinch of ground cardamom
1 vanilla pod, halved and
  seeds removed
10g (¼oz) salted butter,
  cubed
2 tablespoons whipped
  cream (optional)

Preheat the oven to 140°C (275°F), Gas Mark 1.

Place the milk, rice, sugar, cardamom and vanilla pod and seeds in a medium saucepan over a low heat. Bring just to the boil, then immediately remove the pan from the heat. Remove and discard the vanilla pod, then pour the mixture into a deep ovenproof baking dish. Transfer the pudding to the oven and leave to cook, uncovered, for 45 minutes.

After 45 minutes, remove the pudding from the oven and give the mixture a stir. Dot the cubes of butter over the surface of the pudding, then return it to the oven and cook for a further 35 minutes, until all of the liquid has been absorbed and the rice on top has turned a light golden brown.

This is best enjoyed lukewarm or cooled, so set the pudding aside for at least 30 minutes before serving. For added indulgence, fold the whipped cream through the pudding before serving.

# Classic Chocolate Mousse

*Chocolate mousse is easy to make but always feels decadent and sophisticated, which makes it the perfect make-ahead dinner-party dessert.*

**serves 6**

250g (9oz) good-quality
  dark chocolate (at least
  70 per cent cocoa solids)
70g (2½oz) unsalted
  butter
6 eggs, separated
cocoa powder, to decorate

Place the chocolate and butter in a heatproof glass bowl over a pan of barely simmering water, ensuring that the water does not touch the base of the bowl. Leave on the heat, stirring continuously, until the chocolate and butter are melted and glossy. Remove from the heat and set aside for 5 minutes to cool.

Meanwhile, place the egg whites in a large bowl and whisk to stiff peaks with an electric whisk.

Once the chocolate mixture is cooled, add the egg yolks to the bowl and whisk to combine. Now add one-quarter of the beaten egg whites to the bowl and fold in to loosen the mixture. Add the remainder of the egg whites and carefully fold in until fully incorporated. It is important not to be too vigorous here or you will knock the air out of your mousse. Place in the fridge for at least 4 hours to set.

When ready to serve, spoon a large quenelle of the mousse onto each serving plate and decorate with sifted cocoa powder.

# Apple Cake

*The apples in this cake make it deliciously moist, ensuring that it keeps well and can be enjoyed over several days with a relaxing afternoon cup of coffee.*

**serves 6**

80g (2¾oz) unsalted
  butter, softened, plus
  extra for greasing
300g (10½oz) self-raising
  flour, plus extra for
  dusting
1 egg, beaten

150g (5½oz) caster sugar
3 'Cox' or 'Bramley'
  apples, peeled, cored
  and chopped into
  bite-sized pieces
whipped cream, to serve
  (optional)

Preheat the oven 180°C (350°F), Gas Mark 4. Grease the inside of a deep 20cm (8 inch) round cake tin with butter and dust the inside of the tin with a coating of flour.

Whisk the egg and sugar in a large mixing bowl until pale, then add the butter and continue to whisk until fully incorporated. Sift the flour into the bowl, then add the chopped apples. Mix until all of the ingredients are fully incorporated and then pour the batter into the prepared cake tin. Transfer to the oven for 30 minutes, until the cake is well risen, golden and springy to the touch and an inserted skewer comes out clean. Leave to cool for at least 10 minutes before removing the cake from its tin.

This cake will keep for several days, but is best enjoyed lukewarm from the oven with whipped cream on the side.

# Cherry Clafoutis

*This dessert is always impressive, yet is deceptively simple to make. Beautifully sweet cherries are only available for a couple of months every year, but that just makes this classic dish even more special.*

**serves 6**

1 tablespoon salted
  butter, for greasing
150g (5½oz) fresh
  cherries, stoned
3 eggs
seeds from 1 vanilla pod

140g (5oz) caster sugar
1 tablespoon soft brown
  sugar
60g (2¼oz) plain flour
215ml (7½fl oz) whole milk
pinch of salt
icing sugar, for dusting

Preheat the oven 180°C (350°F), Gas Mark 4 and grease the inside of an ovenproof baking dish just large enough to hold all of the cherries in a single layer with butter. Lay the cherries in the base of the dish and set aside.

Place the eggs, vanilla seeds and both sugars in a large bowl and whisk together until well combined. Sift in the flour and salt and mix to combine. Pour in the milk and whisk to a smooth batter.

Pour the batter into the prepared baking dish over the top of the cherries, then transfer to the oven to bake for 35–40 minutes, until lightly risen, golden and an inserted skewer comes out clean.

Dust the clafoutis generously with icing sugar and serve warm.

# Tarte Reine Claude

*This delicious dessert is the perfect middle ground between a summery fruit tart and a warming winter pudding. Greengages are a type of plum that are common in France, but can be harder to find elsewhere. Other stone fruit would work just as well.*

**serves 6–8**

**For the pastry:**
100g (3½oz) unsalted
  butter, at room
  temperature
100g (3½oz) caster sugar
1 egg and 2 egg yolks
200g (7oz) plain flour

**For the filling:**
1 egg and 1 egg yolk
80g (2¾oz) caster sugar
25g (1oz) plain flour
75g (2¾oz) finely ground
  almonds
pinch of salt
225g (8oz) crème fraîche
500g (1lb 2oz) greengages,
  stoned

To make the pastry, place the butter and sugar in a bowl and mix until pale, light and fluffy. Add the eggs and egg yolks and mix to incorporate. Sift in the flour and mix to form a soft pastry. Wrap the pastry in clingfilm and transfer to the fridge for 2 hours before using.

While the pastry is chilling, preheat the oven to 180°C (350°F), Gas Mark 4.

To make the tart filling, place the egg, egg yolk and sugar in a large mixing bowl and whisk until pale and airy. Sift the flour, ground almonds and salt into the bowl and whisk to combine. Add the crème fraîche and whisk the mixture until smooth and well combined. Set aside.

Once the pastry has finished chilling, roll it out on a lightly floured surface to a thickness of 5mm (¼ inch). Line a 23cm (9 inch) loose-based tart tin with the pastry, then line the pastry with greaseproof paper and fill with baking beans. Transfer to the oven to blind

bake for 15 minutes, until lightly golden, removing the greaseproof paper and baking beans for the last 5 minutes of cooking.

Lay the prepared greengages in the base of the pastry shell, then pour over the filling mixture. It's nice if a few of the greengages are peeking through the filling after cooking, so you may want to keep a few back to place on top. Transfer to the oven for 25–30 minutes, until golden brown and lightly risen.

Leave the tart to rest for 10 minutes before removing from its tin. This is delicious served warm from the oven or left to cool and served at room temperature.

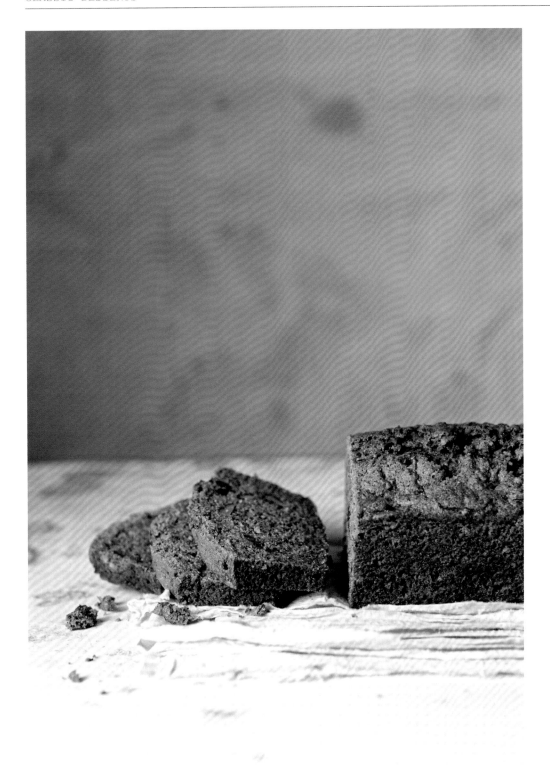

# Carrot Cake

*This delicious cake is packed with chewy dried cranberries and crunchy pecans, while the carrots make it incredibly moist and bring a natural sweetness. This recipe makes two loaves, because one is never enough!*

**makes 2 loaves**

butter, for greasing

**For the dry ingredients:**
125g (4½oz) plain flour
125g (4½oz) wholemeal flour
1 tablespoon baking powder
150g (5½oz) golden caster sugar
1 tablespoon bicarbonate of soda
1 teaspoon salt
2 teaspoons ground cinnamon
1 teaspoon ground ginger
1 teaspoon ground nutmeg
seeds of 1 vanilla pod

**For the wet ingredients:**
4 eggs, beaten
400g (14oz) carrots, grated
150g (5½oz) chopped pecans
50g (1¾oz) dried cranberries
300ml (10fl oz) melted coconut oil

Preheat the oven to 180°C (350°F), Gas Mark 4 and grease 2 × 900g (2lb) loaf tins with butter.

Sift the flours and baking powder into a large mixing bowl, then add the rest of the dry ingredients. Stir to combine, then make a well in the centre and add all of the wet ingredients. Mix everything together until well combined and divide the mixture between your prepared loaf tins. Transfer to the oven to cook for 45 minutes, until golden, well risen and an inserted skewer comes out clean.

Leave the cakes to cool in their tins for 10 minutes before turning out onto wire racks and leaving to cool completely. Serve at room temperature.

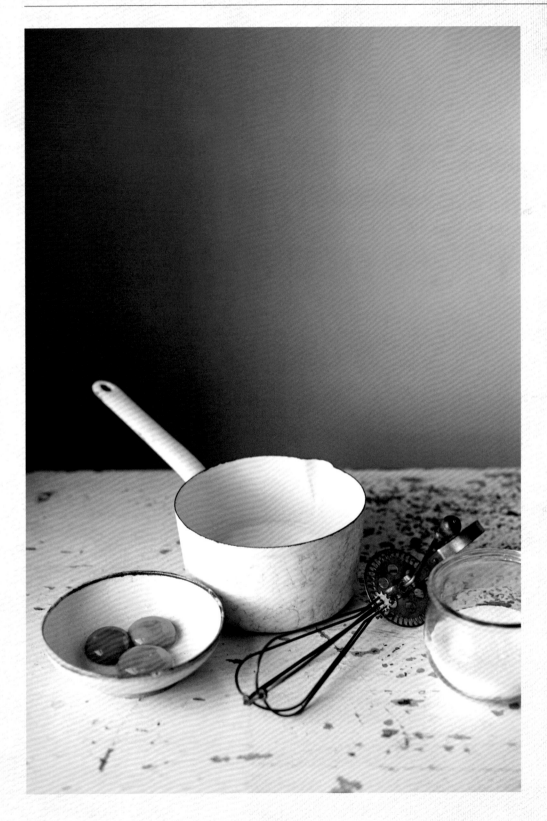

# Chocolate and Aubergine Pots

*This updated version of a classic chocolate mousse requires a bit of a leap of faith, but the results speak for themselves. Aubergine may seem like a very odd addition to a dessert, but its bitterness perfectly complements the silky dark chocolate.*

**serves 6**

1 large aubergine, peeled
  and cut into 2.5cm
  (1 inch) dice
160g (5¾oz) good-quality
  dark chocolate (at least
  70 per cent cocoa solids)

**For the crème anglaise:**
150ml (5fl oz) whole milk
150ml (5fl oz) double cream
3 egg yolks
30g (1oz) caster sugar

Preheat the oven to 180°C (350°F), Gas Mark 4 and line a baking sheet with greaseproof paper.

Spread the aubergine over the prepared baking sheet and transfer to the oven for 25 minutes, until soft and pulpy. Transfer to a blender and blend until smooth. If the mixture is not perfectly smooth, press it through a sieve to achieve a smooth purée. Set aside.

To make the crème anglaise, place the milk and cream in a medium pan over a low heat. Bring just to the boil, then immediately remove from the heat. Set aside for a couple of minutes to cool slightly.

Meanwhile, place the egg yolks and sugar in a large mixing bowl and whisk until pale and frothy. Once the milk has cooled slightly (if it is too hot it will scramble the eggs), gradually pour it into the egg mixture, constantly whisking, until fully combined. Pour the

mixture back into the pan and place over a low heat. Using a kitchen thermometer, continue to whisk the mixture until its temperature has reached 82°C (180°F), at this point the mixture should have thickened slightly.

Break the chocolate into another large mixing bowl and pour over one-third of the crème anglaise, stir until the chocolate has almost melted, then add another third and stir to combine. Finally, pour in the last of the crème anglaise and stir until fully combined.

Add 250g (9oz) of the aubergine purée to the mixture and stir until fully incorporated. Divide the mixture between 6 ramekins and transfer to the fridge to set for at least 2 hours before serving.

# Index

chocolate
  chocolate and aubergine
    pots 293
  chocolate-filled brioche
    245
  classic chocolate mousse
    282-3
chorizo
  fregola, chorizo and
    roasted pepper salad 54
  roasted kale with
    cannellini beans and
    chorizo 135
churros 268
clafoutis, cherry 286
cobia
  grilled cobia, garden
    peas, radishes and
    black butter 131
coffee
  duck breast, white
    asparagus and coffee
    200-1
coriander
  butternut squash, garlic
    and coriander soup 30
  pork loin, carrot
    'spaghetti', roasted
    parsnip and coriander
    condiment 138
courgettes
  green booster soup 18
  'honeycomb' courgette
    cannelloni 116
  stuffed courgettes 77
  *tian de legumes* 66
crayfish
  Japanese seaweed salad
    with crayfish tails 169

D
duck breast, white asparagus
  and coffee 200-1

E
eggs
  individual summer
    tartelettes with a
    quinoa crust 136
  *le Crespeou* 73-4
*escargots à la*
  *Bourguignonne* 78

F
faggot 80
fennel
  roasted onion, fennel and
    pesto tart 100
fregola, chorizo and
  roasted pepper salad 54

G
gastrique sauce 200
*gâteau de Savoie* 264
goats' cheese
  'honeycomb' courgette
    cannelloni 116
  roasted beetroot salad
    with confit shallots
    and goats' cheese
    shavings 43
  spinach and goats' cheese
    quiche 105
granola, gluten-free 127
green booster soup 18
greengages
  *tarte Reine Claude* 287

H
hazelnuts
  gluten- and dairy-free
    blueberry and hazelnut
    muffins 130
  gluten-free granola
    127
  hazelnut and blueberry
    cookies 280
honey
  classic honey madeleines
    267
'honeycomb' courgette
  cannelloni 116

I
Irish soda bread 231

J
Japanese seaweed salad
  with crayfish tails 169

K
kale
  confit pork, kale and
    kabocha purée 214-15
  green booster soup 18
  roasted kale with
    cannellini beans and
    chorizo 135

L
lamb
  'honeycomb' courgette
    cannelloni 116
  spring lamb chop with
    garlic and mint sauce
    107
*lapin à la moutarde* 88
lardons
  split pea soup with
    crispy lardons and
    croutons 27
  white pizza with lardons
    and crème fraîche 102
*le Crespeou* 73-4
leeks
  green booster soup 18
lentil, confit tomato and
  fresh herb salad with a
  mustard dressing 58
lettuce
  grilled baby gem and
    gizzard salad with
    pickled radishes 52
lobster ravioli with a
  parsley condiment and
  bisque sauce 147-8
lychee and coconut panna
  cotta infused with
  kaffir lime leaves 179

M
mackerel, pan-seared, with
  cucumber tagliatelle 208
madeleines, classic honey
  267
meat loaf 106
minestrone with orzo 22
*mini-cannelés Bordelais* 278
mother dough 228
muffins 130
mushrooms
  'honeycomb' courgette
    cannelloni 116
  lapin à la moutarde 88
  *le Crespeou* 73-4
  meat loaf 106
  mushroom agnolotti 189

# Acknowledgements

Thank you to Charlotte and Andrew who got the ball rolling and guided us through our first steps. We are also grateful for Jinny's help, who assisted us in putting the appropriate words to our never-ending family stories.

This book wouldn't have been the same without our fantastic group of girls. Helen, Rosie, Ellie, Linda and Jen made this experience extra special. Our lunch feasts during the shoots will never be forgotten.

Finally, we are thankful to all our friends and family that helped us by sampling every single recipe in this book.

Hopefully these recipes won't be pinched by... you know who.